OVERCOMING
ADVERSITY
BREAKING
LIMITS

BERNARD O. APPIAH

ISBN: 978-9988-2-6082-8 (Hardback)
      978-9988-2-6191-7 (Paperback)

For enquiries contact the author:
Email: otopah01@yahoo.co.uk
twitter: Dr_Otopah
Instagram: drotopah
facebook: BernardO

Printed in the UK.

Lightning Source (UK) Ltd

Chapter House

Pitfield

Kiln Farm

Milton Keynes,

Buckinghamshire

MK11 3LW,
United Kingdom

Ingram Content Group

1 Ingram Blvd

La Vergne, TN 37086

United States

Lightning Source Australia PTY Ltd.

1246 Heil Quaker Blvd

Unit A1/A3 7Janine Street VIC 3179
Australia

Design: *Print Innovation (www.print-innovation.com)*

Dedication

*To my mum, the late Florence Yaa Agyeiwaa Agyen Frempong
(1953 - 2015), you taught me how to deal with adversity.
You will always be in my heart.*

Aknowledgements

To members of The Life Word Centre and the Kingdom of Christ Ambassadors Churches, thanks for your love and support for the assignment.

Bishop Bernard Sallah, you've been a brother. Indeed, iron sharpens iron.

My wife, LadyPastor Julie, you are a blessing. My children, Chrysta, Faith and Leon, thanks for challenging me to greater heights.

My sisters Anita and Pearl, you've had adversities of your own, but through it all the Lord has been faithful.

Mr. Daniel Annan, my book publishing consultant, you made the project easier, faster and enjoyable. Accept my sincere appreciation to you.

THE NARRATIVE

"Now Peter and John went up together to the temple at the hour of prayer, the ninth hour. 2 And a certain man lame from his mother's womb was carried, whom they laid daily at the gate of the temple which is called Beautiful, to ask alms from those who entered the temple; 3 who, seeing Peter and John about to go into the temple, asked for alms. 4 And fixing his eyes on him, with John, Peter said, "Look at us." 5 So he gave them his attention, expecting to receive something from them. 6 Then Peter said, "Silver and gold I do not have, but what I do have I give you: In the name of Jesus Christ of Nazareth, rise up and walk." 7 And he took him by the right hand and lifted him up, and immediately his feet and ankle bones received strength. 8 So he, leaping up, stood and walked and entered the temple with them – walking, leaping, and praising God.9 And all the people saw him walking and praising God. 10 Then they knew that it was he who sat begging alms at the Beautiful Gate of the temple; and they were filled with wonder and amazement at what had happened to him." (Acts 3:1-10)

Introduction

Human beings are bound to face times of adversity in life, and this is what makes life what it is. It seems as though difficulties, challenges, and limitations are part and parcel of the human equation without which would be incomplete. It is incontrovertible that challenges will always surface to incapacitate you, disorient you, and disorganize you in pursuant of your personal goals and attainments, whether it's in your career, professional or domestic endeavours. In fact, Job of the Bible epitomises this existential reality of human life by saying that the existence of the human is short but full of trouble. To describe adversity with standard vocabularies such as pain, problems, challenges and its inevitability in human all endeavours would be an understatement, as it poses a potential threat to the course of human advancement dependent on the time, space, and context at any given time.

The inevitability of adversity means that there must be both general, specific and tested ways of dealing with them. It is, for this reason, the scriptures present us with various stories, anecdotes, lessons, principles, and precepts to handle adversities and limitations.

It is therefore essential to understand that how you respond to those problems with the necessary tools, as those challenges and setbacks will determine whether you bring to accomplishment your engagements. The weight of one's problems, challenges and adversities determine the size of one's destiny but how you handle them would establish if you can fulfil that destiny.

It, therefore, goes to say that whether the challenges, problems, and adversities are small or big, these are experiences that make an impact on your life depending on how you manage them ultimately. For example, when you fail in a particular area of your life or on any undertaking, you have a choice to decide whether you would want to avoid that instance or similar instances altogether or devise another way of confronting the same situation or undertaking for the desired result. The outcome may be either be a self-imposed limitation or a learning experience giving you the platform for higher accomplishments in the future. It is also imperative to mention that there are limitations that can also be imposed by nature. Also, restrictions can be imposed by individuals and even society as a whole, demon spirit entities, loved ones and enemies alike who mean well or otherwise who try to tie you down by saying, "You can't do that!" or "I can't see you in that role." All these may work through individual channels and doorways into your life. These channels and doorways may include previous good and bad experiences, your mind-set and established thought processes and the environment as we may see from chapters of this book. Whether these limitations are self-imposed, people-imposed, nature-imposed, or demonic, an element in dealing with them may involve your effort, courage, self-determination, an adjustment to your self-perception and esteem. And the need for a general understanding of the role that God plays in assisting His children to overcome their adversities and limitations.

Meet The Man At The 'Beautiful Gate.'

There was a particular man in the Book of Acts of the Apostles, who was lame from his mother's womb; this made it difficult for him to live the kind of life he was supposed to live. He was someone who may have accepted his condition as his fate for a couple of apparent reasons and resorted to asking for alms. Some of the reasons may be because at that time in history; there was no proper adjustment made in society for the disabled if it was with obtaining jobs, accessibility to certain public places and legislations against discrimination of the disabled on the job market to name a few. To be disabled was to be resigned to a life of misery and dependency on the largesse of people without having full control of one's life and destiny. The disability impaired his movement and for that matter had limited choices to opportunities society could present to him. This un-named disabled man had lost all hope of walking, and for that matter, a better life probably like his peers in society at large who had flexible terms of choices to determine the course of their lives, until   he met Peter and John at the "Beautiful" Gate. The highlights of the story are as follows:

- Peter and John went up the hill to the temple to pray.

- An unnamed man with a physical disability was asking for alms.

- The disabled man begs for alms from Peter and John.

- Peter and John respond by asking the disabled to fix his eyes on them.

- Peter and John claim they have no silver and gold but power in the name of Jesus Christ.

- They lifted the man up, and he starts walking and praising God.

- There were witnesses to testify of the healing of the disabled man.

In the above highlights from the biblical narrative, Peter and John healed a disabled man who sat at the gate "Beautiful" asking alms from people. It is unknown from the writer of the narrative how long the man has been coming to that location asking for handouts. The main reason why he might have chosen that place was the number of people that went into the temple daily to pray. Peter and John recognised that, what the lame man needed in his life was not the alms he was asking from them but a breakthrough of his limitation. The encounter with the Apostles paints a picture of the difference between wants and needs. The un-named lame turned beggar wanted money, but what he needed was the healing power of Jesus Christ. The few bucks he obtained by begging brought minimal benefit. With his few small coins he probably bought food to prolong his miserable life another day. He needed to deal with his limitations.

Dealing With The Limitations

It is my theory based on the analysis of the context of the narrative, that the disabled begged as a relief from his adversity of being unable to meet his daily needs. The fact is this, if he could sort out the underlying limitation that produced the challenges and adversity he faced he could permanently solve the problem. Peter recognised this misplaced priority with the disabled and tried to focus the disabled's attention on a permanent solution. The intention of the Apostles was to assist the disabled to take care of the feeling of rejection when refused alms by passers-by. And also to deal with the indignity of having to depend on much youngerpeopleoreventheworkingclasshecouldequally have rubbed shoulders with in the social, political and economic marketplace. Healing was the alternative to wasting away in spite of his dreams, visions and the enormous potential he had, to make something greater out of his life. In return for his request for what would have potentially helped him maintain the status quo, Peter offered him a solution and a source of benefit meeting the undiscovered and unrecognised core need. The duo thought quickly, through faith in Jesus Christ and the subsequent power from Christ, the beggar could be healed and enjoy the dignity of earning his bread and many other things that have been inaccessible to him due to his limitations. One of the things that we need to know when we want to come to the place where God has prepared for us is to be able to break every limitation that has been the birth mother of the various challenges and adversities we encounter in our daily lives. The daily challenges and adversity the un-named beggar had, were a result of his disability. His disability was the limitation that produced the challenges and adversity he faced on a daily basis in the context of his era and time. It may sound weird for a twenty-first century person, as different adjustments are made in society to integrate the disabled as much as possible, to realise their God-given potential. It was not so during the era of this biblical narrative. God has a purpose and a plan for everything that He created; particularly His children, for us to walk into it, there are not only obstacles, but sometimes we have adversity produced by certain underlying limitations to confront and to conquer. When we even look at the story of the people of the biblical Israel, God gave them the land which will be flowing with honey, yet they were in captivity in Egypt which was the limitation. Besides their inability to freely possess the land promised them, they had to be engaged in inhumane service as slaves under daily tasks masters. And until God through Moses removed the limitation there was no way their adversity and challenges would be conquered, and begin their journey to the land given to them through promise.

It goes to say that though God has a plan and a purpose for you, it does not mean that you will not have difficulties or problems as you move from where you are at present to the place where God Himself has purposed that you should be. It is therefore critical to understand that the problems or obstacles have underlying limitations. Removing the underlying barrier will make dealing either with the adversities and challenges much easier and straightforward. And growth occurs in different areas of your life as part of the process of dealing with them.

The Growth Process

If you look critically at the life of the un-named disabled man turned beggar, he experienced the reality of power in Jesus name. It was a situation he taught was hopeless and probably could not overcome. His reaction said it all. He was by himself leaping and praising God. It is an experience that he would carry with him all the days of his life and bring to bear on future limitations and its concomitants of daily challenges and adversity. In a future occurrence, he would be less perturbed or moved in a similar instance, knowing that power in the name of Jesus would break those limitations. And also be in a position to teach and help others through his experience to come of out similar situations. Before we assume this to be a mere conjecture, there have been instances in history with God's dealings with His people we can fall on to this enduring fact in this particular case.

The life of Joseph made us recognise the importance of seeking God, even more, when things are getting worse. Joseph knew the Lord would bless him because of his dreams. So he endured many adversities with the limitations of imprisonment, but with patience he overcame. Adversity helps you to develop and grow as a person. By seeking to develop these character traits, we can face those trials that come our way and overcome them with the same strength and grace that Joseph had. Most of us have dreams. However, some occurrences prevent us from achieving such dreams and ambitions in our lives. Like this lame man who sat at the gate of the temple called Beautiful, most of us live in beautiful houses, homes, drive posh cars and eat tasty foods but have limitations to confront. The reality of life in a beautiful place with ugly problems epitomises the ambivalent nature of limitations. You can live in a nice house, eat excellent food, drive a nice car but have nasty problems. Many people look beautiful on the outside until they speak to you, you will never believe they had such problems.

"And a certain man lame from his mother's womb was carried ..." (Acts 3:2). Some diseases might have come to the man when he was in his mother's womb. He did not call for it or negotiated for it but it came upon him, and he had to live with it. It was a limitation in his life because if he wanted to do anything; he had to fall on the help of others. It was very embarrassing to be in such a situation. I believe even if he had to attend to nature's call, someone will had to help him. He was a man with ambitions and dreams with no way of realising that in his current situation. Some of us might have inherited some limitations in our lives. There are people who are born into families with genetic diseases which they did not negotiate in any way to have such illness or come to such family with chronic diseases. It is something you have no control over, hence it is a limitation.

Some people are born into families and in particular geographical locations of the world which are so poor with little opportunity to pursue their dreams. There is nothing so painful and disconcerting in life to have a vision and potential to do well in life but lack the appropriate support systems to realise that potential. They did not negotiate for it, and life has brought it upon them. As some people may put it, the vicissitudes of life has brought it upon them, and they need to be able to deal with it to become all that they have to become.

Some people had a low level of education because their parents did not see the need to sacrifice and pay to take them to a good school so that they can become all that they have to become. It has, therefore, become a limitation which has made them unable to access certain opportunities. So they may be faced with having to work in unstable low paid jobs. Like the beggar, they came out of their mother's womb with a limitation. There comes a time in life that we need to move beyond the limitation that life has brought to us. You might have born into a situation, which you did not ask for, negotiate for or which you did not have control over. It is up to you to decide whether you want to stay with the situation or move out of the situation. One thing that I want to assure you is that it is always possible if you want break out of the limitation. If you want to break out of the restriction, it is possible.

Never make an excuse like, 'if my dad had not died I would have gone far'. What you need to know is that whether you like it or not, your father is dead and he will never come back. It is a limitation. You are left with your life to live; you must be able to make something meaningful out of what life has presented you. It is, therefore, time to be able to take your life into your own hands and be able to do something about it. You need to go up into the realm of God to receive your breakthrough. Do not sit and complain, go up.

As indicated throughout this section, this book focuses on using the biblical narrative to espouse principles and its practical application to overcoming life's many adversities and limitations. It draws principles from three perspectives; the view of the Apostles, Peter and John, the angle of the un-named disabled man and the point of view of someone analysing the content of the narrative for the purposes of knowledge, information and inspiration for living. You will discover through the in-depth analysis of the story, understanding required for daily triumph; affirm already known principles and personal resolutions of the past otherwise overlooked with time, and deploy the information and wisdom from the pages to assist you to conquer your adversities and limitation.

Contents

CHAPTER ONE

GO UP

During the biblical era in question, this particular temple and places of worship, in general, were erected on hills so going to the temple would mean going up the hill. The fact of building temples on hills holds a fundamental principle in the relationship between humankind and God. It is a matter of historical interest that because of the perspective that the people held of God as a Supreme Being and as a being above everything, therefore, a dwelling place for him has to be on high ground. And that was what it was in those days. Also, there is a lot of biblical evidence to suggest that people worshiped on hills and mountains and some were considered sacred places. God, for instance, instructed Abraham to go to a mountain to offer Isaac as a sacrifice. Again, the interaction between Jesus and the Samaritan woman is another example. God told Moses on several occasions to meet with Him on mountains (Exo 4; Exo 19). Isaiah prophesied about God's church and that it is on a mountain that the church would be established (Isa 2:2). The transfiguration of Christ in the presence of Peter, James, and John took place on a mountain (Matt 17); and rhetorical the question of the Psalmist, "who may ascend the hill of the Lord....? (Psalm 24:3). There is a suggestion that mountains and such elevated places probably because of its solitude, and the effort it takes in separating oneself from the masses to reach its peak, creates an impression of seriousness to fellowship with God out of the ordinary. In the biblical context from the Old Testament to the time of Jesus Christ covered by the New Testament, it was within the consciousness of worshippers and believers that they met with God in solitude and for most times this was on hills and remote sites.

In the context of the biblical narrative, the Apostles Peter and John were going up the temple at the time of prayer. The Apostles going up signified taking an elevated position to meet with the Lord, giving themselves the opportunity to reach out to a higher being to acquaint themselves or to seek help or to even recharge their spiritual batteries. Therefore, to go up is either to reach out to God and also to reach out to something above you. Also, it is to take an elevated position to gain a better perspective of situations, events and things around you. It is important to acknowledge that the meaning given to the action of the Apostles Peter and John – going up, is crucial for anyone dealing with the adversity of some sort and battling limitations. We would explore the various perspectives of going up as in drawing closer to God, to break into the realm of God for a supernatural encounter. And also to view things from an elevated position above adversity or limitations as a way of successfully handling them.

Getting Close To God

Jesus in His interaction with the Samaritan woman at the well clarified that people worshiped previously on mountains for the reasons already explained at the beginning of the chapter. However, the time was coming and even near when people will no longer have to go specific geographical locations or mountains to offer worship or meet with God, but rather anyone by the medium of the Holy Spirit could make contact with God anywhere anytime without any restrictions. And that was what Jesus meant when He said, 'the hour is coming, and now is when the true worshipers will worship the Father in spirit and truth.'

It is therefore important to know that until you know how to go up – getting close to God, you cannot confront your problems. The scriptures state that Jesus Christ is the invisible image of God, the Father (Colossians 1:15) and therefore you cannot know the Father but through Christ. In other words, you cannot have a relationship with God independently of Christ because Yahweh is a Holy God and does not entertain any form of un-holiness, as humankind became unholy due to sin through Adam and Eve. The act of sin was the reason why they hid away from God in the garden of Eden. So sin became the element that separated man from his creator – Yahweh. It had to take a man to purify Himself to become sinless to be able to approach Yahweh. God commissioned laws about 615 of them as part of that process till His ultimate sacrifice for cleansing was ready, but the weakness and the proclivity of man to sin meant that it was impossible for man to be able to restore his fellowship with Yahweh through the law of Moses. So in the fullness of time, God sent Jesus Christ, His Son to the earth to die for humankind so that through him we could access God and fellowship with Him as before (Galatians 4:4-7).

And that is why we pray in the name of Jesus or through Jesus because He is the only one in the sight of Yahweh qualified to access Him. So no one can ever go to God directly on their merit, being the righteousness required to qualify to access Him, we can only do so successfully through Jesus Christ. Therefore, to draw close to God would mean building a very close relationship with Jesus Christ, through faith in His perfect birth, the sacrifice of death on behalf of humankind and eventual resurrection, where He's seated at the right-hand of God the Father making intercession for us (Romans 8:34). If we are in Christ, then we can through Christ draw closer to God.

Having said that, there is always need to know how to draw a clear distinction between knowing the existence of God and how to draw close to Him. You can have God in your imagination and never experience Him in your life. God is the God of the physical as well as God of the spiritual. That is why in the beginning God created heavens and the earth. A demonstration of the fact that as a spiritual being He wields control over the physical realm too by creating out of the spirit, a physical place that is habitable by men whom He created in His image to be His vice-regents.

"In the beginning, God created the heavens and the earth." (Genesis 1:1)

God created both heavens and earth so that He can have physical interactions with people in the land. That is how surprisingly personal the creator of the universe can get with those who approach Him through Christ. For a man to establish this closeness with Yahweh, it is essential to remember that He is a person and therefore desires all things any entity as a person may want. This requirement may include, Having times of talking and fellowship

(Prayer). I must say that this talking is a two-way activity - where one talks to God and also listens to Him.

Practicing a time of worship. It is during a time of worship that you take time out to Thank the Lord and tell Him of all the wonderful things He has done for you. We worship with words, with music and a heart filled with gratitude. We enter into an intimate fellowship with Yahweh with thanksgiving and praise (Psalm 100:4). You read and meditate on His instruction – the scriptures. When we study the Word of God, it's important we make the necessary time to be able to think through and mutter the word to ourselves and even memorise it (Joshua 1:8). The more we keep the Word in our minds and hearts the more our thoughts, actions, and character are shaped by the content of the Word which is one of the persons of the Godhead.

We express our closeness to God through our willingness to yield entirely to Him and His counsel. Jesus was precise and straight to the point about maintaining closeness to God through Him. He has stated that we remain in Him and He in us is the key. He used the vine and branches of the vine to illustrate this over- arching truth. The branch that is disconnected or cut of cannot take advantage of the plant food carried by the tree's vast network of conduits which consist of xylems and phloem tissues. And would eventually die from its disconnection. Therefore, the branch that wants to continue to be part of the process of growth must be fully connected to the stem and yield to the course of receiving from the trunk.

Closeness to God in dealing with any adversity cannot be negotiable considering that He is Almighty and we depend on Him in all situations; we can survive anytime if we strengthen our relationship with God making sure that we are well connected and close to Him at all times. Until you know how to draw close to God, break into His realm and dwell there, your adversity will always overwhelm you.

Breaking In And Staying In The Realm of God
Drawing close to God through Jesus Christ is not a physical activity because God is a spirit. And so to draw close to God carries within the understanding of having a spiritual connection to the realm in which God lives. We get a glimpse of the atmosphere and state of that realm in the story of the Annunciation (Luke 1: 26-38). In the interaction that took place between the angel and Mary, the angel's response to Mary's question of how could it be that she a virgin would conceive a child, the angel said '...for with God, nothing shall be impossible...'. The word *with* is a preposition that expresses accompaniment. Therefore, if the angel says nothing shall be impossible

with God, then he's saying that impossibility doesn't dwell in the realm where God lives, and so are those who choose to live in the realm of God.

It stands to reason then, that when you draw close to God, big problems become small, adversity becomes nothing but an opportunity for God to show His glory once more. The reason we see the problem smaller is not because the big problem has shrunk in size or the adversity has lost its destructive potency but because you have taken an elevated position where you can identify the problem with all its dimensions. Taking a high position makes you realise that the problem is small. That is why in the book of Acts, Peter and John were going up to meet with God in the temple, traditionally designated as the dwelling place of God and therefore meeting with God. They were not going down, but they were going up into the domain of God, making an effort to break into the realm where impossibility has no place.

Often, when the policemen are chasing criminals on the road, either on foot or by car, the criminal sometimes can outwit the police in the pursuit. They could just negotiate a curve, and the police will pass, but when the police can no more find them, they will call on the assistance of the police helicopter. The police helicopter by the advantage of being above everyone else in the sky can detect where these criminals have hidden or are on the road. On occasions where the chase occurs in the night, they often use night vision cameras from the skies. The success from the air is mainly because as always when you look at things on the same ground level, they will always overwhelm you but when you take an elevated position, they become small. You do not get lost in life when you get closer to God and move to the realms where God is, situations do not overwhelm you there. Situations overwhelm you when you look at them from the same level as you are. You need to learn how to draw closer to God.

As already hinted in the introduction of this book, to break through your problem in life, you first have to deal with the limitation that creates the problem because the limitation is the cause of the problem. And this can be achieved when you position yourself above the restriction to deal with it. That is to take an elevated position; going up into the realm of God.

There is an African adage that says, 'you cannot successfully pluck away driver ants crawling on your body while standing amongst them where they are gathered.' The meaning is that if you want to get rid of a situation, you may have to remove yourself from the problem to solve it. In other words, the same level at which you create problems is not the same level you solve them. You will need to step up to a higher degree in the process, whether it is with the thinking, the analysis, and drawing solutions.

Aside from dealing with adversity and solving problems from an elevated position of God's realm, you will also able to develop a vision for your life. Thinking big, dreaming big and developing a big idea, it all possible from your place in the realm of God. When you do not have a vision but draws closer to God, you will get a vision for life. The reason is that you will begin to see yourself the way God sees you in all your abilities and strengths and the availability of God's help to accomplish something beyond you.

Vision is always based on your purpose, and God determines your purpose. Whatever purpose you were born for on earth you do not choose it. God has already predestined you to accomplish that. The vision is based on a mental image of what the end will be and the responsibility of how to work it out for it to happen. Some people lament that they do not have a vision because they were not able to achieve what they previously set. It may be that it was not the purpose of God. In an instance you are sure, you just have to keep on working at it. When you draw close to God, you can have a vision for your life.

> *"For My thoughts are not your thoughts, Nor are your ways My ways," says the Lord. "For as the heavens are higher than the earth, So are My ways higher than your ways, And My thoughts than your thoughts."(Isaiah 55:8, 9)*

The realm of God is greater than the realm in which we live. The thoughts of God, the ways of God, are higher than humans and as the heavens are also higher above the earth so it is. In other words, the operations of the realms which God operates are in a higher form and dimension than the realm of humankind.

It is therefore prudent that if you align yourself with God in the realm in which He lives, you position yourself higher above everything. That is why the Scriptures reveal that when Jesus Christ died and ascended to heaven, He sat at the right-hand side of God the father with all the principalities and powers under His authority. He was living in the realm of God. We can also live in the realm of God although we are still in the physical realm. We need to draw close to God to be able to deal with the challenges of life. Until you get to that stage; going up, you will always think that you are at a disadvantage while faced with adversity and limitations.

If you even consider David's approach to defeating Goliath, it stands on this same premise that He didn't look at his physique and personal ability but shifted the battle to the spirit realm where He knew His God reign supreme by saying to Goliath he comes against Him in the name of the Lord. In his own eyes from the realm of God, he saw himself bigger than the giant Goliath. How well you manage life is dependent on the realm from where you are operating and for that matter how you see things. You could always achieve greater things, and significant problems can be solved, you can overcome adversity and break limitations when you take an elevated position by breaking into the realms of God by the process of drawing closer to God. We need to align ourselves with God; move closer to God, and nothing will overwhelm us. The realm of God is where we allow God to lead us instead of controlling ourselves, our abilities and thoughts in our frailty. The Lord wants us to begin to do what it takes to enter into His divine presence because great things happen in the realm of God. Let me sum what we have discussed, are the benefits of drawing closer to God or operating from the realm of God.

Things That Happen In The Realm Of God Impossibilities Become Possibilities

The first thing that goes on in the realm of God is that impossibilities down here on earth become possibilities   up in there and therefore limitations are removed. When Mary had an encounter with the angel in the Gospel of St. Luke account popularly called the Annunciation, Mary doubted the possibility of her giving birth since she had not seen any man yet, but the angel of God said that with God all things are possible.

34 Then Mary said to the angel, "How can this be, since I do not know a man?"35 And the angel answered and said to her, "The Holy Spirit will come upon you, and the power of the Highest will overshadow you; therefore, also, that Holy One who is to be born will be called the Son of God. 36 Now indeed, Elizabeth your relative has also conceived a son in her old age; and this is now the sixth month for her who was called barren. 37 For with God nothing will be impossible." (Luke 1:34-37)

The word "with" in verse 37 is a proverb which expresses accompaniment. The verse did not read "For God, nothing will be impossible." but "For with God nothing will be impossible."

It means that even if the situation is of impossibility when it comes in touch with God, it turns into a possibility because once it dwells in the same place as God, it must turn into an opportunity. It further shows that whatever problem you have, when you move into the realm of God, the problem is no longer a problem. It is very crucial as Christians to always live in the same realm with God. If you enter the realm of God, impossibilities are possible; limitations are no longer limitations because God gives you the ability to overcome them. You need to go up. You cannot deal with issues when you are at the same level with them.

Someone came to me sometime in the past overwhelmed by a difficulty he was going through at the time. He was at a point where he could see no way out. Options he was considering was more of quitting altogether or committing suicide. I looked at him and said to him "do you know the problem I am going through now as a pastor?" The person said, "oh pastor you are belittling my problem." I started to share one of my problems with him, suddenly, he started crying. He thought the difficulty he was facing was bigger than what anyone had on earth. I had a much greater problem I was dealing with, and yet I had not given up or was I in my house lying bed crying. Suddenly he realised that the perspective you take of the difficulty determines whether you develop the strength to deal with it. Indeed, I had climbed into the realm of God and was seeing my problems from a perspective where I believe they were solvable. The issue is that if you take an elevated position, problems are no longer problems. In the realm of God, all things are possible. If there is any situation of impossibility, limitation or adversity, when it gets in touch with God, all is cut to size because, in the realm in which He lives, there is no impossibility or limitation. That is why the Bible says let the weak say I am strong (2 Corinthians 12:10). This sort of positioning when you say you are rich, when you are poor can only be based on understanding the Word of God from God's realm.

Before the assassination of Dr. Martin Luther King Jr. in1968 in Memphis, Tennessee, he delivered 'I have a dream' speech with a portion that read;

"And I don't mind. Like anybody, I would like to live a long life - longevity has its place. But I'm not concerned about that now. I just want to do God's will. And He's allowed me to go up to the mountain. And I've looked over, and I've seen the Promised Land. I may not get there with you. But I want you to know tonight, that we, as a people will get to the Promised Land. And so I'm happy tonight; I'm not worried about anything; I'm not fearing any man. Mine eyes have seen the glory of the coming of the Lord."

In the above speech, Dr. Martin Luther King Jr. expressed the struggle they have gone through to get to where they were. Though he may not get to the mountaintop with them, he knew their struggle would never have been in vain because before that Malcolm X, had been killed in addition to other leaders of Civil Rights Movement. He was aware that his time was up. King's thoughts were obviously on his mortality. However, he was not afraid because he saw the victory ahead, his view was from the top of the mountain. When you take an elevated position, problems do not overwhelm you. When you move into the realm of God, struggles seize though it may be difficult now you once in the realm of God you would not struggle with your difficulties.

You Develop A Better View Of Life And Destiny

When you enter the realm of God, you develop a better view of your life and destiny. Sometimes when we go through difficulties and hard times, we question the provision of God for our lives. Some of the issues may be how a loving God can allow this child to suffer like this? Or if God loves me why am I suffering? Some even stop attending church. The problem is that you are looking at the problem from the level the problem was created; you need to move up. When you move up, you will be able to get a decent view of the problem.

Some of us encounter little difficulties, and that overwhelms us. What you need to know is that every problem that you face is temporary, because the Bible says only the Word of God shall abide (1Peter 1:25). If the problem, adversity, difficulty is not the word of God or anything that does align with the Word of God it will not last. Sometimes you may be in a particular situation, and it is getting worse but never give up because the higher you go, the better view you get. As you move into the realm of God, you will understand your situation better. No wonder most people say in the end that they now know why those things did happen to them. They had moved to a point where they can now have a proper view. And what overwhelmed them in the past, don't now?

I had a friend who failed GCE 'O' Level English. She sat for the exams again and failed. Fortunately, when she was going to collect her result, I met her. She put the result sheet on the ground and lamented why God had disappointed her on two consecutive sittings. She eventually decided to rewrite for the third time. It was during the second re-sit she met her husband. Her husband was her friend's brother who had returned from Europe at the time and was on the school campus to pick up his sister. The gentleman took the lady with him to Italy after they got married. If she had passed the exams, this would not have come to pass. It is therefore important to know that you do not have to understand everything but you need to move to the realm of God to be able to comprehend what it is God is up to. In the realm of God every situation of adversity, present within it an equal measure of great opportunities.

You should not be bothered about the delays you are going through because you do not have an idea of what God is preparing for the duration of the delays for you. The day that He decides to open the gates, you will experience a supernatural overflow in your life.

Step Up Of Thought Patterns

Again, when you enter the realm of God, you develop thought patterns that are higher than the normal human thought. When you enter into the realm of God, you do not think as other people think and consequently, your lifestyle also follows suit.

When people are afraid to take a step in a particular direction because they are waiting for some natural occurrence to confirm their movement, rather, you are already moving because with God all thing are possible. You are not waiting for a physical manifestation to confirm your action because you are not thinking like other humans. We need to be able to come to that place; where the way we think, the things that we say conform to the things which happen in the realm of God. Even when you wake up in the morning and you have a head ache, you should not be filled with fear because you said when my mother was about to die she experienced the same thing. You need to think and process information like God; if you do, some occurrences and adversity that comes against you may not scare you. Do not stay down and complain, think and act like those without a God. If God has spoken, He will bring all that He has spoken into physical manifestation. When God speaks, you do not need to have a second thought, just obey. And this applies to almost every area of life.

In the realm of God, you develop healthy thought patterns; you do not think as the ordinary human being will think. Many people may believe that this cannot be, but you will say, with God, it can be. It is this thought pattern; Peter wanted to demonstrate by asking Jesus to let him come to Him on the sea (Matthew 14:22- 29). He stopped thinking about the laws of gravity and relative density and just stepped out into the water until he began to think typically like a human again considering all the impossibility of walking on water. In the realm of God, when God speaks all things are possible. We have to learn how to enter into the kingdom in which He is so that we begin to enjoy life the way He wants us to enjoy. However, living in the realm of God does not mean you will face problems, difficulties, and adversities as I demonstrated to you in the previous section with the story of the gentleman who came to see me. But you will be able to handle them differently because you are up there with God in His realm – thinking like He thinks and seeing as He sees. When you come to Christ, it does not mean problems ceases to exist in your life, but if you enter God's realm, then you could see them well, think through them well and be in a better position with God's assistance to solve them or overcome them completely. I hope you have now made up your mind to enter into the realm of God because of the abundance of the existence of His mercy to be applied to all the problems in your life.

To continue with the summary of the important points raised in this chapter let's look at the process of entering the realm of God.

How To Enter Into The Realm Of God Learn To Meditate On God's Word

Meditation is pondering over the Word of God in our hearts, preaching it to our souls, and personally applying it to our own lives and circumstances. The word of God contains eternal divine wisdom held in the shell of personal vocabulary. God wants to "break open" this shell of human vocabulary that contains the infinite divine wisdom and begin to discover the abundant wealth of personal application and the understanding that they hold for you. The realisation of the effect of the Word can be accomplished as you memorise and meditate on the word.

The Apostle Paul once said,

> *"Let the word of Christ dwell in you richly in all wisdom, teaching and admonishing one another in psalms and hymns and spiritual songs, singing with grace in your hearts to the Lord." (Colossians 3:16).*

Meditating on Scripture will cause Scripture to "dwell in you" and become a source of wisdom in your mind, will, and emotions. Through that, you will be able to break every yoke with the word. Similarly, the Book of Joshua and the Book of Romans also indicate the benefits of staying one's mind on the Word of God and meditating on it.

> " This Book of the Law shall not depart from your mouth, but you shall meditate in it day and night, that you may observe to do according to all that is written in it. For then you will make your way prosperous, and then you will have good success."
> (Joshua 1:8)

"For to be carnally minded is death, but to be spiritually minded is life and peace." (Roman 8:6).

Always keep your mind on God's word. It is what your mind contains that control your life. If your mind is full of God's Word, God's Word commands your life, and if God's Word controls your life, you'll live in freedom and prosperity. If you keep your mind on your problems, your problems will control your life such that you can be happy or free to live life to the fullest. There have been people who have stayed their minds on their problems and been overwhelmed by it and thought the only way out is to commit suicide. Others have resorted to the use of narcotic drugs to supposedly numb the pain of the problems they face to no avail. In the end, it has a toll on their health and wellbeing. Such people tend to look older than their real age. Considering the effects of choosing other things, events and circumstances to dominate our thoughts, it is always prudent to keep your mind on God's word rather than on your problems. Spend time on God's word.

Another Biblical fact to support meditating on God's Word regularly and consistently is the fact that, apart from the Word whose incarnation is Jesus Christ, it is the tool the Father uses in getting anything done. We know from John 1:1-3, He (the Word) is the same essence and glory like the rest of the Godhead (Father and Holy Spirit), He was at the very beginning with them, and all things were made through Him, and there isn't anything carried out without Him. Therefore, when we read and meditate on the Word of God, we empower ourselves through the creative abilities of the person of the Word to accomplish great things with our lives. In other words, we unleash the Word and all of its unlimited properties and features into action in our lives. Thereby, transforming us, and the things that surround us bringing them into conformity with the Word. In other words, the realm of the Word is extended beyond the pages of the scriptures through our mouth and absorbs everything in its environs and establishes its authority and reign over all.

Martin Luther, one of the pivotal figures of church history, gave detailed instructions on how to meditate to benefit from it. He taught that;

"You should meditate not only in your heart, but also externally, by actually repeating and comparing oral speech and literal words of the book, reading and re-reading them with diligent attention and reflection, so you may see what the Holy Spirit means by them".

We are pressed for time in each day and even more so when in our contemporary time we declare time is money. Meaning, you can exchange your time for money. Broadly speaking there are things money cannot buy. When you trade your time with meditating on the Word of the Lord, in return you reap the benefits discussed in a couple of paragraphs above.

Never invent excuses for yourself; create time to meditate on God's word. Get a study guide such that every day you read and have the word in mind. Someone once said that he does not listen to the news or read his letters until he has read the word of God, meditated on it and prayed. Without the word inhabiting you, you could be easily disturbed by life's circumstances and difficulties that surround you.

Every individual that has an experience with the practice of meditating on God's Word would tell you that. I have been through problems, but I trusted God that He is able. There came a day where we had nothing in the house for the family not even for my little daughter at the time. But standing on His word, He supplied. You do not need to focus on the problem but meditate on the word of God.

As an expansion to what Luther taught on the effective ways to meditate I present to a few suggestions, you could consider with your daily practice of meditation.

Ways to meditate on God's Word:

- Take time to read a verse or passage over and over.
- Begin to memorise all or part of it – speaking it yourself.
- Listen—quiet your heart to allow the Holy Spirit to speak to you through God's Word.

- Consider how it fits with the rest of the Bible and life in general.
- Become emotionally involved—allow yourself to feel what God feels, his desires expressed through his words.
- Move from meditation to application—connect your thoughts to action. Consider how the truth and power of the Word of God should affect your behaviour.

Speak The Word

The next point to enter into the realm of God is to speak the word of God. It was God who said let there be light, and it was so (Gen. 1:3). It was God who created stars (Gen. 1:16) and put them in place by the utterance of His mouth; it was according to His word. That process of creating and controlling the environment in which we live has not ceased. Let me discuss this with you on two levels;

The World And All In It Is Controlled By Words

We need to understand that because God created the worlds and everything in it by the words of His mouth given to us in the form of the scriptures, the world and everything in it only responds to the Word of the Lord. There is no language that the world and all created things understand but the Word. However, what we want the world to be is dependent on what we speak into it. It is the words that we speak that shapes the world in which we live. If we choose to speak the Word of God which ultimately defines the direction of our world in alignment with God's Word, then we benefit but suffer if it is otherwise. I have seen how stock market decline or go up just based on speeches from influential world leaders. Economies are boosted or otherwise just by the utterance of words by some of these leaders of the world developed economies because investors seem to make their decisions on the prospects of their investments in a particular industry or country as a whole based where they think that industry or country is going. And come to think about it, it's all just words without action. Words that can change significantly and yet it either puts fear into people or gives them hope and consequently induce actions which may affect people trans-generationally.

People take arms against each other because of what is said. Even people commit suicide just because of what they heard. Words are crucial, it controls our World, and it's even more potent when it is the Word of God from which the world was created. Creation bow to the voice of God's Word. One thing to note, which I discuss at the second level, is who is speaking it.

Speaking The Word By Those Filled With The Spirit Of God

Those who follow God through Christ Jesus have the ability to recite the same powerful word that God used to bring the universe into existence because we have the person of the Word in us and works through us. When we speak of the power of the Holy Spirit, the Word which we are speaking is brought into manifestation because the realm of the Word takes over and absorbs everything else. It superimposes Himself upon our environment. When we speak the Word we release technically we release the person of Christ into action. We need to note that the time of creation (Genesis 1:1-3), God spoke "let there be light and there was light" at the time when the Father spoke the Spirit was moving upon the face of the deep so in partnership they produced the light into the world that was very chaotic. The essence of the light which was a combination of the Word and the Spirit's activity having been released by the Father, was to bring clarity for the other actions to be taken. When we speak out the Word of the power of the Holy Spirit, we release the person of Christ into our environs. And we learned earlier on in the chapter, when God steps into any life, any situation with impossibilities and failures give way.

Instead of speaking about your problem and rehearsing it to yourself, rather speak the word into the situation confronting you. You need to search and find scriptures that speak the Word that is in line with your problem. That is why it is always good to study the word so that you know the appropriate Word to speak to the power of the Holy Spirit, to manifest it in your life. To clarify the above point with an illustration, if you have bills to pay and you just speak the word hoping it will nullify it, it won't happen. Your prayer would not be to make the law non-existent but rather activating the Word of the Lord to make way for you to make money to sort out that bill. I have to say that this is not in place of one finding a job or even being a very good manager of finances.

But rather when all these are in place, and one is behind and needs a way out of a tight financial situation. The reason I say when all things are in place or rather use an economics term 'all things being equal' is that examining the scripture below throws more light on this factor. I know that believers quote this Philippians 4:19 but most also misquote and misappropriate it, in the sense that the context was about another church that has sent supplies to Paul the Apostle, in his time of need. So it is a promise appropriated on the condition of having fulfilled your religious obligation or having the lifestyle of supporting God's work here on earth.

One thing I see that happens if we speak negative words over ourselves; we will get results of those words which will be what we don't want. That is the power of our words. But again, if we speak the Word of God on a day to day basis; we are opening the door for the supernatural in our lives as did the centurion, and our Lord and the many recorded examples in the gospels.

I would encourage you to make a lifestyle changeright now, with the way you speak to focus on speaking into your life the Word of God which has inherent power to transform and change your life. If you are facing any adversity in your life, have any limitations in your life that you need to remove, they would be eliminated speak to them just like Jesus said we should.

Act On The Word Of God

In the realm of God, it is not hard working that makes people successful, nevertheless hardworking is not discounted. That is to say that in spite of the fact that speaking the Word of God allows the realm of the Word to take over it must be followed by acting on what the Word says. So like Isaiah 55: 11 puts it;

> *"So shall My word be that goes forth from My mouth; It shall not return to Me void, But it shall accomplish what I please, And it shall prosper in the thing for which I sent it."*

The Word carries enough inherent power to bring itself into manifestation as its realm absorbs, take over the environs spoken into and expresses its reality through that context of the expression. However, Jesus used the illustration of the wise and foolish builder to illustrate the difference between those who hear or read the Word and do what it says and those who hear or read but do not practice it (Matthew 7:24-28).

Acting on God's Word should of equal measure complement the Word that we speak either through meditation or deliberate pronouncements into particular situations. Do not just praise the word when you hear it being preached or when read, but begin to act on it so that you can see the manifestation of it in your life. Through faith we act, we can act on the word of God that we hear so that we will see the actual manifestation in our lives.

We could go to church every weekend and listen to Bible readings and sermons being preached and feel very spiritual because we are listening but without acting on it or practicing it would not benefit us. When we do that, we are like   the people who go to a health club or a gymnasium and watch people exercise. That does not get you healthy or build your muscles. Reading and listening to God's Word without acting on it, will not make you more spiritual either. It could make you appreciate the benefits thereof without being a partaker. It is not enough to just say that you agree with what God's Word says on a subject. You must do it. God's Word is meant to be acted upon.

> *"But be doers of the word, and not hearers only, deceiving yourselves. But he who looks into the perfect law of liberty and continues in it, and is not a forgetful hearer but a doer of the work, this one will be blessed in what he does" (James 1:22-25)*

You would realise from the Book of James as quoted above that, those who receive an eternal blessing by being exposed to the Word are those who take the next step of acting on the Word and practicing them. Acting on the Word is an indication to God of an individual's reliance, agreement, and faith in His Word as being genuine and eternal. And for that, God honours His Word in the lives of those that do that.

Fast And Pray

Fasting and prayer is the most powerful combined spiritual exercises available to the believer. Fasting has been an ancient practice as a religious rite in many religions around the world. The hint of the efficacy of the power of fasting was given by Jesus when someone brought their child to the disciples for healing. After an unsuccessful attempt to deal with the issue, they passed on the case to Jesus who said that 'this kind does not go except with fasting and prayer' (Matthew 17:21). The process of fasting involves denying the body of food and other pleasures while concentrating on prayer and the study of God's Word, through that one can break out of the 'flesh – carnal nature' and partake in spiritual things in the realm of the Spirit. That is to say, that true fasting brings humility and alignment with God. Humility in the sense of subduing the desires of the flesh and the Spirit of God is given free access to have His way in your life during fasting.

It breaks the power of flesh and demonic influences. It has the potential to kill unbelief as one's sensitivity to the Spirit of God increases. Consequently, this ensures we receive answers to our prayer when under normal circumstance with prayer without fasting, we may be found wanting due to the enormity of the spiritual obstacles confronting us.

Prayer is not a preparatory element for the battle over our limitation – prayer and fasting are the battles in some sense in the life of some believers. Once you win the battle over exercising yourself through the act of fasting and prayer, you're guaranteed some amount of results. And of all the things we can do to enhance the power and focus of prayer, fasting is doubtless the most potent. Fasting puts us in harmony with an all-powerful God who demands humility from those who wish to be close to Him. Fasting humbles the flesh and allows God's Spirit to have His way in the life of the individual. Prayer and fasting for the purpose, of humbling oneself please the Spirit of God.

You can walk with God and experience many things, without fasting much because I am not saying fasting is the only thing that opens you up to the efficient working of the Spirit, and grants you access to the corridors of spiritual power. However, the highest, richest and most powerful blessings and ability to go up to the realm of God is by fasting. The most significant Biblical characters were all men and women of fasting and prayer. Jesus, the Son of God, was a man of fasting and prayer (Matthew 4:2). So was the Apostle Paul (2 Corinthians 11:27). Moses fasted 80 days. Elijah fasted 40 days. The early church fasted before starting any major work. Those characters mentioned in the scriptures without any indication of fasting might fast because it was a common religious practice at the time.

The greatest spiritual leaders of the 20th century who are making an impact are all men of fasting and prayer to my scriptural knowledge. Anyone who started a significant religious movement in Christianity was, to the best of my knowledge – Martin Luther, John Wesley, Charles Finney, John Knox, Robert Evans, William Seymour and William Booth were all men who acknowledged fasting as a spiritual exercise. If done right, fasting counts a lot with God. Fasting is however not magic, nor does it twist the arm of God, but as already emphasised it creates room in the life of the individual for God to work with and through them. God wants to do many amazing things, but He looks for those willing to urgently make the corrections needed to come into alignment with Him so that He can lift them up like how the lame man was raised. God resists the proud but gives grace to the humble.

Fasting among its many benefits provides you with a focal point of reference for your life, which is dependence on God. It is a major key to hearing God's voice. We need focus on God more than anything. The world we live in is working overtime to distract us, to entice us, to win our hearts, minds, focus, and to give us an alternative vision. Fasting helps us to disconnect from the world and its distractions so we can tune into God. If we are obedient to God, fasting will be the needed catalysts for tapping into the exceeding greatness of God's power to overcome all forms of adversity and breaking through all limitations in our lives. Ironically, there are many instances in the bible when on both personal and national levels, individuals and nations have resorted to fasting, and the Lord heard them and came through mightily for them, bringing an end to one calamity or adversity of some sort. It is a difficult exercise, but considering the benefits, it makes it worthwhile to make the sacrifice. Doctors sometimes, advise patients to fast before a particular blood test, a scan or for some detailed medical examination. Patients comply as part of the process of diagnoses, prognoses or treatment, then any individual that wants the strength to deal with any form of adversity or limitations should be ready to go on this journey of fasting.

Worship
From the scriptural perspective, the act of paying honour to God with reverence and homage provides access to the enclosures of the secret places of God. To quote Psalm 100:4, "Enter into His gates with

thanksgiving, And into His courts with praise. Be thankful to Him, and bless His name."

The court, as quoted from the scripture means an enclosed pasture for feeding. Enclosed pasture for feeding today is a dining room of a monarch, or even of a family. One notable thing regarding enclosures for food is that it's a private area for close members of a family and their associates. Until you have an excellent relationship with the host be it a monarch or a particular member of the household, you may not get an invitation to dine in the privacy of their home. And in so many instances, significant issues are discussed during that time of dining; peace comes about; strategic family decisions are made; discussions of proposals to progressive endeavours and other gestures of goodwill such as exchanging gifts takes place. As an adage goes, a way to a person's heart is through the stomach. We should understand giving honour to God through reverence and paying homage, grants us access of fellowship with him, to hear Him and be heard. The fellowship in His presence is what thanksgiving and praise do for the believer in Christ. And this is part of the worship, considering that in worship we express our approval and admiration of God, His nature, character, and acts; and express our gratitude and devotion for blessings received.

To qualify the above assertion, the word worship from its colloquial rendering is worth-ship. In the context of our discussion presupposes offering reverence, homage and honouring God according to His worth. As we do this the Lord, in turn, admits us into His presence, and we accrue to ourselves all the benefits there is to gain by dwelling in the secret place of God. The good news is, we can gain access irrespective of the time of day into the courts of God to have fellowship with him.

We should learn as believers how to worship God. We should not only worship God when we attend churches but in our private moments of solitude too. When you develop an attitude of worship, you always remain and live in the realm of worship. Worship catapults you into the realm of God as we may have realised because, to talk about the private chambers of God, the place of dining for a monarch is the same as such. We get an insight of the nature of worship from Psalm 22:3; "But You are holy, Enthroned in the praises of Israel." As you worship God and give Him praise and honour, he steps into His praise, in other words, that offer draws him, and as He approaches with the beauty and splendour of His glorious presence, we are absorbed into the reality of His realm. God is always looking to His people through whom He can showcase His power enabling them to overcome their adversities and break through their limitations. To enter His realm that makes all this possible, one needs thanksgiving and praise packaged through worship to the Lord.

CHAPTER TWO

AT THE GATE: CARRYING SELF

Sometimes, you may meet people in your church or the shopping mall and wonder if these people do not have problems because they all seem to be about their business. People have learned how to put smiles on their face but beneath the cute and beautiful faces are a lot of problems some of which are killing them slowly.

In the disabled beggar's story, it is not clear how He got to the places where he begged for alms or in this particular story how he got there. There is a possibility that the man was carried every day to the gate of the temple, considering the level of technology at the time and other indications elsewhere from scripture they carried people in that sort of situation. He found himself at a place where he could get help to meet his daily needs because of the challenge of obtaining a job to earn a living, notwithstanding the fact, that wasn't going to take away the limitation that was producing the problems in his life. The temple was a place where people go and seek the face of God, with the possibility of miracles occurring, the motive of the disabled beggar sitting at the Beautiful Gate was short of breaking

through his limitations. Over time his expectations have been to deal with the daily challenges he faced. And so nursed and managed his infirmity as much as he can. Ironically, he was so close to a miracle or God himself and yet he had problems. He was in a place itself called 'Beautiful' and yet had an ugly problem to contend with in his life. If it was the case of where he was usually carried to the place of begging for alms, it is true to say that, there comes a time in life that some people by now should be walking but cannot. Some people are carried by others through life when they should be doing well in life. They have to depend on other individuals to live a meaningful life. It is not what they want, but the circumstances of life have imposed it on them as a condition with a little way out momentarily. Unfortunately, in life, there are people who through certain natural deficiencies, or accidents, or false accusations, have certain conditions imposed on them. They may not be the cause and yet whether they like them or not the limitations have been placed on their lives. There is no clear indication from scripture as to what the cause of the disability was, but we assume it was a similar case of nature imposing the limitation on him without his involvement in the process. He might not have contributed in any way to the events that led to the condition imposed on him but had to deal with it anyway.

How Do You See Yourself?

There is no trivialising the conditions the disabled beggar found himself in, considering the limited resources and opportunities available to him in his day compared to a lot of people in our time who would not find his kind of disability a limitation. Being carried by others to sit at the Beautiful Gate to beg for alms speaks volumes about the way he saw himself. His estimation of himself played a significant role in the actions he took to deal with his adversities and limitations. How the disabled beggar saw his past, present and future determined the way he chose to live his life. In addition to the point made above, disabled people of the twenty-first century could be considered more productive and accepted by society. Society recognises disabled people for their potential and ability to make meaningful contributions to the development of their communities. The social response to the change in the way disabled people are treated now came on the back of a challenge to the status quo. It was to enable them to see themselves outside of the box from which for centuries disabled people saw themselves. It might have become standard in national life for the opportunities and perception we may have of disabled people. However, it started from somewhere when someone realised his or her worth was more than society tagged them to be. How do you see yourself? Whether your adversities are nature imposed, self-imposed, demon-imposed, how you see yourself would play a significant role in your eventual triumph over them. In other words, you must own your life, and you must carry yourself and be responsible for how your life turns out.

There is no doubt that living with limiting beliefs can force you to live a mediocre life that is far away from your real potential and therefore, learning how to identify and get rid of such self-limiting beliefs is the best thing you can do for yourself. You need to have an incredible faith in yourself. It must be an idea based on the fact that your creator made you special and that you possess abilities when properly harnessed can catapult you into fulfilling your purpose here on earth entirely. Within the context of dealing with adversity and limitations, it takes a strong belief in one's ability to be able to know you have what it takes to get through with it. You need to know who you are and believe in your abilities, acknowledging your weaknesses and managing both in any given circumstance.

By becoming self-aware and understanding your strengths and limitations, you open up opportunities, become honest and have genuine relationships because the people that you are attracted to, will be attracted to you for who you are. The problem with limiting beliefs is that they usually seem inconspicuous to the extent that most people find them very hard to identify because it is within your sub-consciousness. A person can hardly tell whether his or her deeply rooted belief is the limiting factor.

It is alright to be born with a limitation or to have restrictions imposed upon your life, but it is not alright to live with a constraint for the rest of your life. You have the responsibility to be able to breakthrough that limitation and move forward to achieve the things you want to achieve and reach the heights you want to reach. Many people would not have wished to be born into the families in which they are because of congenital diseases and other troubles in those families. What you have to remember is that you can break every limitation. You can break every barrier if you know how to handle it. Every person in one way or the other is born with a limitation. Limitations are the core problems that produce the challenges we have in our lives. If you go to the hospital and complain to the doctor you have a migraine, the pain in the head could mean so many things other than a migraine. It could be a symptom of malaria, typhoid especially in tropical areas, brain tumour, and even cancer, etc. That is why the doctor will not immediately administer any drug to you but may undertake a prognosis to help him unravel the real disease and its cause to prescribe a remedy for you subsequently.

Some years ago, I lost my one of my elder sisters in Ghana. She had intestinal perforations as a result of typhoid. In her case, she was experiencing "go slow" which was a local parlance given to the symptoms of malaria where one could feel alright in the mornings but have a terrible fever in the evenings. While battling the disease, during the day time, she was alright, but in the night she had chills. The symptoms persisted with different prescriptions until she started experiencing pain in her abdomen. Doctors diagnosed her of Intestinal Perforations as a complication of typhoid and therefore required an emergency surgery. My sister passed away a night before she could undergo surgery. Typhoid which was her limitation brought many challenges to her. We could not identify the deficiency early but rather dealt with the problems it was producing. The import of this anecdote is that it is worth getting to the bottom of all circumstances past the challenges to break through the limitation as the big deal.

One of the problems among humans is that we do not know or understand who we are. That is why there are a lot of theories trying to explain the self and identity of humans and their relationship with one another, which have sparked confusion in the minds of many people. We need to know who we are. We have been wired by the creator to withstand severe challenges and limitations that confront us. The clue can be found in various flora and fauna;

and creepy crawlies; and animals in their different habitats. We know for instance about mimicry which broadly refer plants and animals respond to the adversity and dangers in their environments for self-preservation.

We as humans should be able to define who we are by what God wants us to be, through the purpose He has given us to fulfil. Who we are is not determined by people around us but may be affirmed by those around us. It must be the case because you could find yourself in situations where those around you cannot see anything worthy in you and therefore you cannot depend on them for their affirmation. Beyond people not seeing anything good in you, some could even go to the extent of verbalising bodly their disdain for you, openly making sure that others also recognise that you're a nobody. But the irony of the situation is that sometimes people do that deliberately to put you down due to their insecurities to get even with you. They try to conflict who you are and what they think of you in their head. Choose to believe what God created you to be than what they claim to make you be.

I have conducted job interviews and sometimes come across people who from their CV's and checks have the requisite training, skills and the ability to perform in that particular role and yet perform abysmally during job interviews because they don't even know who they are to let alone believe in themselves. And you come across others who believe in themselves because they know who they are but with minimal skills, and yet are very articulate and carry themselves as though they can fit that role perfectly. Besides, the lack of knowing is affecting your career, there is no doubt that having a self-limiting mind-set would set the cap on your ability to flourish in every given area of life.

It is equally problematic to lose your identity as an individual and as a result, underestimate yourself, or over-estimate yourself. Most of the time when you meet someone who has over-estimated himself, he or she looks down upon people and do no treat people well while other people see such a person as a colleague in every sense of the word. The same way, if someone underestimates himself or herself, he or she is likely to complain about the manner in which people treat him or her. It may be that you are above them and you are forcing yourself down to their level. In life, if you give valuable things to people who do not appreciate things which are valuable they will misuse them. It is like giving gold or diamond to someone who does not know the value of it; it will be misused and abused. It fulfils the common phrase 'cast not your pearls down to the pigs.'

How You See Yourself, See Others And Others See You

Inversely to our discussion in the preceding paragraphs of this chapter, we have been examining how the disabled beggar saw himself, his self-identity and esteem. It is worth noting that how he saw himself subsequently affected how he saw or perceived Apostles Peter and John. Peter remarked on what the lame man saw them to be; whether they have the ability to assist him to deal with his adversity, solve his problem or breakthrough his limitations. The disabled beggar perceived them to be one of those worshippers who would drop some coins into his collection bowl and just walk off to mind their business. To be fair, the gentleman, his experience with worshippers of the past may have also conditioned him to accept his state of being because none might have offered him the opportunity to deal with the situation in which he found himself permanently. His motive with expectation for going to sit at the Beautiful Gate was just to collect from benevolent worshippers some loose change to take care of his needs. He might have lost faith in anything that could reverse his condition and restore him to a place of equity among others within his community.

One day a lady from my congregation came to see me, complaining bitterly about how some rascal guys who want to date her. Her biggest problem was that those guys propositioning her as their girlfriend was not the calibre of people she wants to date. It was a simple case; how she saw herself for who she was made her carry herself in a particular way that subsequently made her attractive to those specific guys who she considers out of her league. I made her understand that these people are after her because she attracts them on the basis of the issues I've raised in this paragraph. Soon that changed when she knew what I meant and made the necessary adjustments to her life.

Another biblical narrative that comes to mind talking about this particular principle; the twelve spies that Moses sent to spy out the land before God's people moving in to occupy it. Two out of twelve spies were the only ones that brought encouraging news, making an effort to align what has been prophesied about and given as a promise with the actual situation on the ground. The two affirmed that indeed the land was promised and they could move in to occupy it. However, the remaining ten couldn't see the alignment of the promise with the situation on the ground, but what informed them of their assessment was the belief in who they were and subsequently how they saw those that were already in the land they went to spy. They saw themselves as grasshoppers, and for that matter, they perceived others saw them as such (Numbers 13: 27- 33). Their response to what they saw in the land was all in their minds, as it wasn't the case. Yes, the Giants were in the land, but it was false to assume that the Giants perceived them as grasshoppers. It is evident through the events that unfolded that the giants that were already occupying the land never recognised them as they presumed. Their thought of how they the residents of the area saw them was not how the inhabitants of the land saw them; the problem was within them. It was a false perception of who they were. And guess what? The responses of the ten spies and their actions after that was that of abandonment of the promised land.

Also, the report from the land of Canaan by the ten spies was very disheartening because it portrayed the Israelites as little grasshoppers in the eyes of the Canaanites. The scouts underestimated the strength and the capabilities of the Israelites except for the report of Caleb. And even more importantly they forgot about the unlimited ability and power of the one who had promised them the land. When He (God) says it, it is what it is although it may not look like a possibility at the time the promise was given. Most of us have that kind of belief and mentality. We do pray but do not have the right mind-set that God can do exceedingly abundantly in our lives. Even though God's promises to us may be barricaded by giants and may look like an impossible situation, Caleb believed God could give them victory over them.

We need to realise that our limitation is a ground for a break, through the agency of the power of the Spirit of God into a new level if we are willing to make some adjustments in our lives. Adjustments like, Changing the way we think, changing the way we talk, changing the way we behave, changing anything that is necessary to succeed in life and ministry. We are all in the process of change; we are being changed from glory to glory even as by the Spirit of the Lord. The Bible tells us that God does not change so we humans have to change and become more like Him, to fulfil our destiny; to become a bigger person, and to achieve more in any area of our lives.

The lesson we draw from some of the biblical narratives and anecdotes in the section of this chapter is that, until you deal with the limitation that exists in your mind about who you are, you are more likely to make a wrong assessment of your adversity and limitations, and deny yourself the possibilities that may be available to you. The limitation in your mind to who you are, tell in your attitude, lifestyle, and choices you make. As the saying goes, 'you are addressed the way you are dressed.' The reason is that the way you dress is an indication of your sense of worth or self-esteem. When someone gives you a seat, and you ignore the dust on it, it speaks volumes of your sense of worth. It does not mean you are humble or someone who lives a simple life except you are probably in a deprived area or a location where you want to identify with your host or community and therefore want to show solidarity. Besides a situation like this, it is a problem if you have to make a seating choice and you choose to sit on a dusty seat even if it was offered to you because you feel intimidated by your surroundings. Your action indicates you have underestimated who you are in the eyes of those around you and you are more likely in the same measure, be underestimated by those around you.

We need to have the right sense of judgment of our situation, adversity, opposition, and limitations to be able to press ahead through them all. We should know who we are, know the supernatural resources through the infinite power of God available to you as against the adversity, limitations, and opposition you have encountered. I picked up from my unusual upbringing and the wider cultural context from which I grew up that people typically ask "what are you called or what do people called you" instead of "what is your name" when they want to know your name. You do not have the opportunity to say who you are. Your judgment of who you are is often based on someone's else opinion of who you are, and therefore in my assessment of the situation, you are more likely to go through life accepting the image that others have of you in their imagination etched on your mind. In that way, you are far more likely to live to fulfil the expectation of others through your attitude, behaviour, and lifestyle.

The greatest small package express service in the world today is the result of a man who refused to accept his college professor's opinion. He was awarded a low grade for a ridiculous concept. He went on to create Federal Express. Many people told a scrawny kid from Ontario, Canada that his size and skating abilities would prevent him from playing professional hockey. He went on to change the NHL and its record books.

He is Wayne Gretzky. As Shakespeare said in act one, scene 2 of Julius Caesar; "The fault, dear Brutus, is not in our stars but ourselves." Self- awareness is essential to the discovery of your power and the defeat of self-imposed limits.

You need to check yourself very well. Many individuals in our world pretend to be who they are not, and others also reciprocate it with praise or disdain. People always want to hear good things about themselves, so it's made others to speak to them of what they want to hear. If you intend to follow the words of people all the time, you will not go far. There are different kinds of individuals in the world and how they see things; some are constructive, some are harsh, and some give little praise without the craze.

Who You Are - Types Of People You Encounter In Life

The Self-indulgent Type.

Every individual who will have to work with people irrespective of the stage and level would encounter these people and would have to consciously make some adjustments to protect one's sense of worth and esteem. They are the kind of individuals that could let you feel worthless and at a disadvantage in every conceivable area of life. These are people you encounter in life who are generous to themselves and so critical of others. They usually make good remarks about themselves and are very harsh on others with every given opportunity. They criticise people all the time but see themselves as faultless. They know how to sooth their pain from disappointments even when it was their making, and yet are highly critical of others in similar situation to theirs. The reason for the above-stated attitude is because they consider themselves important above every other and would put themselves first for any form of relief or advantage in every situation. They do not appreciate people, no matter what they do. They usually see problems, weaknesses, difficulties, challenges, and limitations in the lives of others. These type of people are ungrateful for the input others make in their lives because they overestimate their importance over and above everyone and everything.

In some cases, the very things they discourage others as being insurmountable are the very things they secretly make an effort to overcome. They consider themselves able to accomplish everything they did because they had a unique ability or were lucky enough to have been able to do so. You will need to protect yourself very well if you find yourself among these type of people. Contextualise whatever they are saying or acting within your knowledge of them and draw your conclusions about what the truth or motive may be for that gesture towards you. To escape their venom, you would also have to filter whatever comes from them very carefully to ascertain what is genuine and would be helpful; and what is meant to put you down. Where it is possible you could probably consider cutting off your friendship or whatever grounds that brings you together, if it is at your behest and have that sort of control and choice.

The Unsatisfied Type

Another kind of people you encounter that also have an impact on your sense of worth or esteem are those individuals who are tough on themselves and generous to others. They are the type that strives for perfection and for that matter and are never satisfied with their attainments and achievements.

They have philosophies that work for others well, but they do not have such for themselves. They deal with others nicely. They always want to be seen in the eyes of the populace as humble and being there for others apart from themselves. They find it difficult to complain even if people offend them or when they encounter challenges because to them it makes them feel as though they are a burden. They do not want to be criticised by the people, so they have set a high standard for their lives. It is a case of an underestimation of life. The result of underestimating yourself is that the same people for whom you self-deprecate and debase are likely to take you for granted. There is the need to always draw the delicate balance between avoiding over- estimating yourself and underestimating yourself. The point is to just be who you are.

You should not set standards which are so high that you cannot reach while you have given a low standard for others to operate freely. Someone said that the road to failure is trying to please everybody at the same time. No matter how you conduct yourself to people to get favour and praise, it will never last in their eyes because man's good deeds are written on water while the evil deeds are etched in stone. That is to say, that, know who you are and just be. There is no need to live consciously trying to bring down yourself in the eyes of people to exalt them. You realise that sometimes the very people you do this for do not, in the end, appreciate you in anyway the way they should, rather they take you for granted.

The Wide-Eyed Type

These are people who acknowledge that just like anyone else, they also have strengths, weaknesses, struggles and blind spots. These people seem to be able to draw a good balance between processes in an individual's life and the result. That is to say that when they or others are in any situation, they do a quick scan to find any hidden strengths, weaknesses, struggles and blind-spots that may have influenced the outcome and therefore empathises with the situation. They may not approve the result or consequence, but they do not use their position of strength against the others' position of weakness to get even, to destroy, to undermine or to even differentiate their position.

These people see others from a holistic perspective, and for that matter, nothing surprises them. Having said that, they are very quick to support to restore any lost dignity, honour, and relationship. They are in touch with their humanity, and as a result, they see people as humans above what they do or happens to them. People to them are not a consequence of anything and everything; they are still God's creation and make them a priority above everything else in His creation. Please don't misapply this to mean that those with these attributes are the sanguine type or are all over the place trying to make friends with everyone. They could have any personality type and still be a wide-eyed person, although it is admissible that some personality types develop this attribute or portray it more prominently than others.

It is important to consciously adopt some of these traits of the people in this category if you want to have excellent relationships with individuals in life. If you carry this sense of consciousness, you can deal with your adversity, limitations or challenges without being too soft or hard on yourself. You will understand that there are things you cannot do and there are things that are difficult to do, so you need to know what to expect from others in every circumstance. People in this category do not overestimate themselves nor underestimate themselves; most of the time they have the right disposition at the right time. Finally, we are all created with everything we need to live successfully in this world irrespective of our personality type and its disadvantages. Everything we are exposed to in our environment over time also adds up to what we become and its manifestations in every area of our lives which includes the choices we make every day. Sometimes, we limit ourselves with our choices, and we go away from our true brilliance, graceful potential, and purpose in life. The good news is this: you can get back to make various adjustments in your life to realise who you are meant to be. Genuine happiness and success will be yours when you make a choice to find out who you are; to know, respect, honour and respect your rare individuality. The greatest care and gift you can give yourself is the deep pleasure and knowledge of being able to say: this is who I am, and this is what I want. God always want to prepare a group of people who know exactly who they are. Jesus was able to defeat the devil simply because He knew who He was. He was able to beat Satan at his own game (Matthew 4:1-10).

In almost every area of life, knowing who you are, is vital because it impacts on how others see you through the way you carry yourself around. If knowing who you are and seeing yourself as God has made you, made Jesus succeed against Satan, then without any doubt its good for us to know who we are to enable us to deal with any form of adversity we face and limitations we may have on our lives. Some

Limits In Life That We Must Accept

It is true to say; all human beings fail at some point or the other, whether it is a decision, an action or inaction, a choice, an attitude or way of thinking. Some make a determined, conscious effort to press forward from there to success while others don't. Real success is not avoiding failure but learning what to do with it. Even in a situation a person knows who they truly are, it doesn't insulate the person totally from failure. In a way, these failures in themselves can be limitations on our lives we may need to break in order to move forward. Whatever the failure may look like, it is better to attempt things and fail, than never to attempt anything because you are afraid to fail. We never learn the limits of our ability until we reach the point of total failure. Thomas Edison had tried over five thousand different types of light-bulb filaments before he found one that would work. His willingness to endure many failures gave us the modern electric light bulb.

However, having discussed some of the ways by which we have limitations upon us in the first chapter, it must be made clear that there are some limitations we have just because we are human and nothing more.

There are facts about life as Fred Smith put it, "a problem is something you can do something about. A fact of life is something you can do nothing about. Here are some limits in life that you and I cannot do anything about them.

The Limitations Of Our Days.

We will not live forever to do whatever we may want to do in this world. It is for this reason the Psalmist said, "So teach us to number our days, which we may gain a heart of wisdom." (Psalms 90:12). Our days on earth is limited and there is so much we can do within the period allocated by our creator. It is only wise to accept the fact that, you have allotted time and do not have the luxury of time on your side. All thing must be done within the allotted time. Depending on the perspective, this could be perceived as an advantage or disadvantage the fact that the time is short and no one knows the time of departure as well. Having our days numbered is a limitation from the human perspective because there is a probability that you may not finish everything you set out do in the life of the living. Jesus was mindful of this very fact in His daily routine, work and ministry and so said, "I must work the works of Him who sent Me while it is day; the night is coming when no one can work." (John 9:4). Whatever the case may be, we will one day leave this earth, but that should not deter us from pursuing our goals in life. We should not say we will die, so there is no need to do anything about our limitation. We should ask the Lord for wisdom to use our time effectively.

The Limitations Of Our Gifts.

There is no one in the past or still alive that has all it takes all the time to fulfil all tasks. No one can ever do it all. Apart from the fact that it is deliberately designed to make us all interdependent on one another, to foster respect and love for one another. Similar to our interdependence on one another due to the limitations of our gifts, is also the fact of our dependence on God. Each of us has abilities, gifts, and talents according to a measure determined by God. It is enough to enable every individual to fulfil their purpose on earth and live a meaningful life (Romans 12:3; Ephesians 4:7-16). We understand from the perspective of scripture that, God did not just create one organ he created a whole body with many distinct parts and functions. Each part is meant to play a particular role that together with other areas of the body can get things done. In the same way, one person in the body of Christ cannot do it all. There need to be others involved, each making their contribution to ensure the success of any venture at all. Never be jealous of what others can do more than you but be willing to learn from them if you so admire their pace, dexterity, and mastery. Better still you can learn and apply the principles with which they have developed themselves to replicate their success in your venture or assignment. There are naturally gifted people working the works of God in a particular way you are not gifted the way they are. You can be willing to complement theirs with what you have been given so that together you can achieve more. You cannot do everything, but there is something you could do better than everyone else no matter how small it may be.

The Limitation Of Resources

We all must accept that we have limited resources required to fulfil our tasks at any point in time. Whether it is in human expertise, finances, or talent, we cannot have it all and sometimes have to fall on others or even wait till we can pull all needed resources together before going ahead with a venture.

From our main biblical narrative, we have discussed in this chapter, going up into the realm of God. There has been bits and pieces of information, analysis, and conclusions to assist you in seeing as God sees, think as God thinks and perceive as He perceives to enable you to do business with Him in His realm. Whether it is about knowing who you are, seeing yourself the way God sees you or acknowledging that in spite of all the resources in Christ for you, there are limitations we have just because we are humans. The Apostles John and Peter were going up to do business with God when they chanced upon the disabled beggar. At that point when it depended on them to help him they were able to sow seeds of hope by asking the beggar to look at them.

CHAPTER THREE

LOOK AT US: THE SEED OF HOPE

The disabled beggar when he met the Apostles Peter and John on their way to the temple asked for alms, and instead of just dropping a few coins in his collecting bowl the first statement they made was 'look at us.' It was a call to him to look beyond his present state and for the first time see something different from the psychological point of view. They wanted the disabled to see the hope of being like them. If you like, they presented themselves to him as an archetype or a model of health and well-being for him to re-envision to be like them. They wanted to draw his attention from the self-derived consciousness of himself with all the adversities, difficulties and limitations; he had to see once again the hope of living without his disability. It was a case of, giving him a new mental picture of his future free of the limitations of his present, which could be having a life like that of Apostles Peter and John. Mental images play every important role in the formation of dreams and consequently their accomplishments. Our expectations are created as a result of our mental pictures stored in our sub-consciousness. Therefore, expectations could change when our mental images also change. The disabled beggar's expectations of the Apostles had to change if he was going to receive anything that could permanently alter his way of life forever. They had to let him shift his attention from himself at that moment in time to give him an opportunity to develop a new mental picture of health, freedom, and happiness. And so at that point, the closest the Apostles could get was to ask him to focus on them and look at them. It is probable that the beggar may have been stunned by that bold instruction, and might have been thinking, 'who are these people at all' and so might have truly for once in a split second shifted his attention to these men imagining who these people could be.

And it was obvious they were a bit different to him, a picture of what he might have wished to be but for the right opportunity or possibilities, have been begging for alms to get by in life. What you look and see most often is what you end up becoming. If you see abuse all the time there is a chance you could become abusive; if you see corruption all the time there is a chance you could be corrupt; if with every turn you see poverty, there is a chance you could become poor because mentally all these become your 'normal.' There is this interesting story of a man who went to see a palm reader during a difficult time in his life. During the consultation, he was told that he has obviously been through some tough times in his life. In his exasperation, he asked what next from that day onwards because he wanted to hear great things were about to happen in his life. To his amazement, the palm reader said 'the change that would take place is that you'll become adjusted to the situation that you will no longer require a change. Many people have adapted to various situations of adversity and limitation that they no longer need a change. Those circumstances have succeeded to condition them to see nothing better than what they find themselves in. Sometime ago, I saw a video clip being circulated on social media, which made me cry. The video recording was made by someone in a village of a developing country and involved a group of school children aged between nine and twelve years.

The one who was recording the video asked each of the children what they wanted to become in future and their responses would astound you. Compared to most children born into a family of a developed nation who would say, they want to be a fireman, teacher, doctor, nurse, barrister, for instance, the children wanted to grow up and collect stuff from the garbage dump and sell them, others wanted to be porters in the market. The answer that brought tears to my eyes was the child who said he wanted to be a ghost. I tried to analyse his answer in so many different ways to understand what motivated his reply and what I concluded was that he wanted to escape all the problems around him. He wanted the ability to be visible and invisible when he wants and could without the forces of nature restricting him to his current life in any way. That notwithstanding, it is clear that the environmental pictures these children see all around them have conditioned them in a way not to see a better life beyond. Their mental pictures of life are images of poverty and hopelessness they see all around them. To change their image of a better future is to change their mental pictures. To change their mental pictures would be to create for them a new environment of possibility which may or may not include the change in location but merely controlling their interpretation of the images they regularly see around them. This process would not be a denial of their state but the helping them develop a mind-set of possibility beyond stark existential reality.

Jehovah, did the same to Abraham when he complained to him about being childless and not having anyone to legitimately inherit his wealth, his name and his beliefs to continue with his legacy (Genesis 15: 1-8). For Abraham, there wasn't anything God would do for him that was enough consolation for being childless. It is not clear what the diagnosis might have been, but it was evident something was wrong with Sarah, his wife and could not possibly have children, and Abraham thought that was it. The images of the stars in the night sky was the mental pictureGod showed him to affect his expectations of God.

Even though a while before that, God had appeared to Him and reiterated His promises to him. He couldn't see anything beyond his current state and that troubled God a great deal. He needed to do something radical about the situation since he couldn't see any way out of his lack of a legitimate son. You would not understand if you read this biblical narrative through western European lenses which does not give much attention to the issue of gender and inheritance. However, in ancient Middle Eastern cultures, it was a big deal not to have a son due to the patrilineal nature of societies at the time. There are some cultures around the world that still hold these cultural practices.

As part of the radical move of Jehovah to solve this problem for Abraham, he instructed him to step out of the tent at that time of night and look into the sky. Abraham might have been wondering the essence of that exercise, however, upon responding to God about what he saw in the night skies, God told him that was going to be the number of descendants he was going to have. In other words, you are asking for just one child, but you have more than you can think of or imagine possible. The exercise was to help Abraham get a new mental picture of the future and not focus on his present adversity and perceived limitations to his legacy.

When we juxtapose the earlier narrative of the disabled beggar and the instructions given by the Apostles John and Peter upon Abraham's own experience, one thing stands out; to be in the right place to deal with your adversity and limitations you need to develop a good mental picture for a better expectation. It is important to note that our lives flourish or diminish by the mental images we hold of our life's situations and the future. If we could change them, it is more likely we could change our future too not to mention dealing positively with life's adversity and the limitations that threaten our very existence.

Receiving The Seeds Of Hope

Not only did the instruction given by the disabled beggar's benefactors was meant to change his mental picture to enable him to see the possibilities of change but also they sowed a seed of hope. Hope based on an existing model or archetype of what you would want to be. By asking the disabled man to look at them, the Apostles were creating an enabling environment for what could potentially happen with his cooperation. The Apostles considered sowing a seed of hope in him necessary to overcome the adversity and limitation he had. Hope begets strength, and strength begets action, action begets results. It takes hope to bring about positive change. Hope kills inertia and propels one to take necessary risks for accomplishment. Receptivity to the seeds of hope creates the opportunity for that seed to grow into a tree of hope with the edible fruits of accomplishments.

Commendation goes to the disabled beggar for his receptivity to do what the Apostles were demanding from Him. He had demanded money from them. Then in no apparent move to give him the money such as they pulling money from their money bags or wallets, just stopped for a while and then instructed him to look at them. It is my analysis that if the disabled beggar had insulted them, ignored them or even challenged them, they might have left, and he would have remained in his state, but to the contrary, he was willing to see what the result of the instruction could be. Yes, time and chance happen to all as the scriptures declare, but one must be sensitive enough to be receptive to be considered ready for the seeds of hope to be planted for the inevitable change that follows. It was not a coincidence that at the Annunciation, after the angel had told Mary of the things to happen, after a few questions of clarification she said 'be it unto me according to your word' (Luke 1:38). Although there were details of the prophecy by the angel, it was still difficult to imagine how that was possible, she was still receptive for the seed of hope to be sown in her heart. As a result, the content of the message in its own time and season took place as promised. Again we can relate this issue of receptivity to Mary and her son Jesus at a wedding in Canna (John 2:1-12). We read of Mary teaching the organiser of the marriage a lesson on receptivity. When it was clear that the wine at the function had run out, Mary got knowledge of it and knew her son was in a position to do something about it because she knew his capabilities. However, lack of cooperation could hamper his capabilities to solving their problem. She knew that it is not always the case that when people have problems, they readily recognise the solutions to them because some may appear unconventional. So in order not to truncate the possibility of a miracle she told them just to do whatever Jesus told them to do. In the end, they complied and when they had done what Jesus asked them to do, to fill the jars with water the water turned into wine. They had to be receptive to experience the miracle. The miracle was in the container that held the solutions to the embarrassment of shortage of beverages on such an august occasion. An adversity has been dealt a blow as a result.

Nurturing The Seeds Of Hope

God has planted seeds of greatness in every person, and His plan for your life is for those seeds to sprout and grow and produce in you a life of health, wealth, and happiness. From the very start of creation, it was

God's plan for people to enjoy life. Humans were the ultimate, the highest pinnacle of creation. God did not plan for His creation to be sick, to be poor, and to be in bondage but He rather planned for them to be on top of the world and exercise dominion. Until Satan through trickery and fore-knowledge of human's weakness took advantage of them. Humankind handed over the dominion mandate of the earth realm to Satan. Through the birth, suffering, death, and resurrection of Jesus Christ of Nazareth, we have taken the dominion mandate back. The dominion mandate is the agency of our belief in Christ and appropriating the right principles of this process of restoration. Principles such as the content of this book for instance helps us to rule in life.

Beyond the generality of the seeds of hope and the receptivity, the examples given focuses on verbal instructions in the form of words spoken. There are no words spoken or written stronger than the Word of God

- the Scriptures. The role of the Word is critical because God himself never did anything without the Word. At creation, for instance, He spoke, and it unfolded into reality, and He still does. He never does anything without the Word. Therefore, in dealing with adversity and limitations, you need the Word of God, which God recognises and responds to as amply discussed in the previous chapter.

If you will provide the necessary warmth and the water, the seed need to germinate and grow; then you will enjoy the results that God has promised. It is often the case that we complain without first meticulously exhausting the use of all the spiritual, material resources made available to us to nurture the seed of God in us for greatness. The life of the beggar portrayed someone who was close to the beautiful gate yet he was unable to access the potential remedy he needed for his adversity and limitations.

The lack of recognition of the seed of God, has made people who should have come of age and be living their lives representing what God has made them to be, but are not. There are individuals who because of their education, age and experience should be leading but others are leading them. The beggar has not as yet nurtured the seed in him to blossom. The lack of recognition and nurturing of the seed is the story of the lame beggar at the Beautiful gate. His seed was locked up within without doing much with it all. It would be a mere speculation to assume the beggar never tried. Whether it was easy in his era to handle such an adversity or be dealing with a limitation of that kind, but the bottom line is that a whole life at that time was put on hold and resigned to hopelessness until the Apostles came along.

We acknowledge that life at that time was in no way like it is in the twenty-first century today where there are equal opportunities and policies in work places where the disabled would be employed. The jobs that were there needed a physically abled person, so it was impossible for a person with disability to find work. The only available means of survival was to beg for alms. Even for him to come to the gate to beg for alms, he had to be carried to the location. There are even societies today that have severe difficulties with integrating the disabled when it comes to employment and social mobility. But a day came in his life that he had a miracle that broke through his limitations and the daily adversity consequently shattered in its path.

Using The Seed You Have Received

As the disabled beggar looked at the apostles, what was to come momentarily sounded like a disappointment for all the effort put into focussing on them at their instruction. Probably expecting a huge sum of money dropped into his collecting bowl, but then the Peter said, "Silver and gold I do not have, but what I do have I give you...". The apostle gave what he had to help the lame man beyond his expectation. While the disabled beggar's expectation was at best limited to getting money to get by for another day or two, the Apostle was thinking of breaking his limitation once and for all. They had the seed of God's power through Christ Jesus in them that no adversity or limitation could withstand. Within the context of the narrative, besides all other forms of application which we would get into shortly, what they had within them is the power of God. Every individual born of God through their belief in Jesus Christ has power inside them to deal with every form of adversity and break limitations. When we are born into Christ and subsequently baptised in the Holy Spirit, the experience is a literal submersion into Christ. Meaning, that with every move the power of God could be at work on our behalf enabling us to live as overcomers in all situations. If you want to understand, look at what Jesus said in John 7: 37-39;

> *37 On the last day, that great day of the feast, Jesus stood and cried out, saying, "If anyone thirsts, let him come to Me and drink. 38 He who believes in Me, as the Scripture has said, out of his heart will flow rivers of living water." 39 But this He spoke concerning the Spirit, whom those believing[a] in Him would receive; for the Holy[b] Spirit was not yet given, because Jesus was not yet glorified.*

There is a sense you get of this scripture, of a scene out of a TV show of the work of lifeguards on a shore of an ocean. You sometimes have an instance where someone almost gets drowned in water; the person is quickly rescued and brought out. At that point, the tummy is pressed down so water could come out via the opening of the body. As macabre this illustration may be, it seems to be a good way to try and explain what Jesus said. The rescued took in water because they got submerged in the water, as part of the first aid when you press their tummies down the same water they were submerged in and went into them comes out. With Jesus' statement, because we are immersed in the Spirit and therefore filled by the power of the Spirit with every move, it is the power of the Spirit which breaks out of us to work externally with and for us. When confronted with adversity or limitations you can in the same way as the Apostles administered the power of God to the disabled beggar, face your difficulty and limitations with the seed of God's power you have received by accepting Christ as saviour and being baptised in the Holy Spirit.

Another important point to recognise in this part of the narrative is the contrasting self-knowledge and self-identity of the disabled beggar and the Apostle Peter. The disabled beggar didn't know he could have a better life the way God wants him to have while the Apostle knew what he had and was quick to deploy it to his advantage and the advantage of the beggar. In the process of the Apostles ministering to him, the Apostle made a far more permanent impact on the life of the beggar. The impact could affect his generation and beyond, and also the fact that the demonstration of power in the name of Jesus the way the apostles did give a recognition to their faith as being what it is, and also authenticating the claims and promises of Christ to his disciples doing greater works like Jesus.

You should remember that God wants you to manifest that seed in you. It is what is in you and what God has given you that your livelihood must depend. Livelihood is not all about working hard to acquire degrees or get employed but your ability to make use of what God has given you. Even at your work place, you may be so relevant to the employer but until you can decide how much money or conditions of service you want, you cannot be all that valuable to your company. It is evident in our world that there are those who stand distinguished in their careers that they are headhunted for roles in the job market while others send thousands of CV's to organisations around and get no interviews. It wouldn't be a wrong assertion to make therefore that there are jobs available not everyone can do. Head- hunters go around looking for highly skilled persons for particular jobs because of the scarcity of such skills on the job market. The shortage of expertise and its relation with joblessness is not in any way trivialising the complexity of unemployment, the job market and its connection to national economies. In as much as not all people are the same at all levels all the time obtaining a job also depends on the scarcity of your skill type or the differentiation of your talent on the job market. As a result, those who have differentiated their talents or have skills in high demand command wages with the power to negotiate with those that pick them for the job. To link our discussion on using the seed, the seed is meant to provide you with a hope of the future, it is right to say that if your employer dictates the amount of salary you are to receive, you have not been able to utilise what God has planted in you to the fullest yet. The seed has an endless potential. The limitation to the seed is the extent of your ability to harness its potential for yourself and the benefit of others.

The life of Kathy Buckley is an excellent example of the ability to overcome limitation. Kathy Buckley was born deaf. Her parents told her that she would never be able to read and she would never amount anything, and yet today she is a successful comedian and motivational speaker, not to the hearing impaired but to those who can hear. She has a noticeable hearing impairment, but she has an excellent sense of humour. She always says that one advantage of being deaf is that she is never interrupted by hecklers when she performs, she simply can't hear them.

The time has come for God's children created in His excellent image to know that they are more than what the world is telling them they are. You are worth more than what anyone is telling you. The only person who knows your real value is the one who set your value. What God has given you is a seed, no one else here on earth has or will ever get. God has given you a seed, and that seed is self-determinant, a complete package in itself. Some people want other people to validate them before they self-recognise their value. The typical accolades often used by people include the boss, director, manager, chief, senior, a way of recognition. There are titles carved by men which may not reflect your exact status but to keep up with the protocols of your organisation, but you know you could be better than that with or without titles. The showering of accolades is a deception in the face of God. It is about time you rise and begin to demonstrate what God has given you.

You sometimes come across people from migrant communities who complain about the difficulties of making a decent living in advanced western countries and have nicked-named places where they live 'Babylon,' 'Egypt' and the like. Some even claim that if they had their legal residence permits, they would have been in a better place socio-economically. There is truth in these assertions and desperate cries of these migrants, without discounting the pain of dealing with up-rootedness and the rejection from communities of the host societies, however, it is equally true that the lack of legal resident permit shouldn't be the beginning of the end of one's life. In one vein though not encouraging flouting immigrations rules of any country, if you find yourself in a situation like that you could equally nurture and use your seed and make invaluable contributions to the development of that nation where you are resident.

It is equally true but there are also many people who have these documents and yet cannot do anything meaningful; even the citizens of those countries sometimes complain. It is therefore important for people to know that these legal resident documents do not necessarily create a life for you. It is your ability to use the seed God has put in you that is the key to opening doors for you. God has already given you what it takes for you to make a life out of it; you have the seed to become great. Without trying to sound controversial, even though prayer is one of the powerful tools to   the believer, it does not get all things done. There are things that after you've prayed, you would have to rise to your feet and act, sometimes through sweat and pain. The main thing that prayer does is that it creates the necessary conditions for you to blossom. You have to make an effort after prayer to focus on nurturing the seed and deploying the power of the seed within. Due to the recognition of the seed they had within, the Apostles were able to make it count for the benefit of the disabled beggar. They were men of prayer as its obvious why they were going up to the temple to pray. However, they gave what they nurtured over time, tried and tested in their lives. It was not the silver and gold the disabled beggar expected from them but the seed of the power of God in them to end his adversity and limitations. Your seed can manifest itself too if you are willing.

How Your Seed Can Manifest Itself In Your Life

In the previous session, we had a look at the contrasting self-knowledge and self-identity of the disabled beggar and the Apostles. We discovered that the Apostle used what they recognised from within them to help the disabled beggar. The act is also from the background that the disabled beggar had a seed in him but didn't recognise it, and that is why he resigned to begging for alms. In this session, we would be concentrating on how you can prop up or assist the seed within to manifest. When a seed in you manifest itself, it may not be necessarily taking the step into great riches suddenly. You may not have great riches, but you will

not be in a position of begging for alms to get by in life. The seed can provide you with what you need. One thing that you need to keep in mind is that everyone has a unique seed in him or her that is capable of bringing forth fruit.

Discover, Develop And Deploy The Seed

We have already established; everyone has a seed, but the problem usually is how to discover it. Some know their talents but compare themselves to others to the neglect of God's gift or seed in them. It is never too late to discover what you have and make use of it. Some may be good at playing football, swimming, singing, teaching, writing, etc. but have forced themselves to become what others want them to become. It is the case that sometimes, people are also attracted by the dexterity and aesthetic beauty of what others do and overlook their seed and copy others. Do not abandon your gift given to you by God or be overwhelmed with the challenge of how to start harnessing it. Do not be scared with the responsibility and work you would have to do to potentially leverage your seed. Some people fast and pray for jobs and end up unfulfilled, complaining about the job they prayed for. You may have qualifications which may be in some way assisting you to develop the seed in you. It is never late to retrace your way back to discover the seed and start doing something with it. The truth is that with all your experience and difficulties you've encountered doing other things in the past, developing your seed may not be as difficult as you may be envisaging. I knew someone who was a qualified chemical Engineer. He went to the USA from an African country with the mind-set of not taking any menial job. Pursued further education to the doctoral level in a reputable university. While still in the USA, he bought some chemicals and decided to apply his knowledge in chemical engineering in his kitchen. Lo and behold, he was successful and now has one of the leading cosmetic companies based on the East Coast of the USA. What this man did was to harness his creative abilities to develop the seed that was lying dormant his life but with his new acquired skill and understanding within the field of chemical engineering he was able to develop the seed he discovered within to a greater achievement. His secret was that he used the gift God gave him. Your gift may be starting a small business either alone or with someone. It may be a gift whose kind you've never seen anyone anywhere exhibit; you just have to discover what you have.

When the late Steve Jobs, the co-founder of Apple Computer was once asked about the secret of his success, he said "your time is limited, so do not waste it living someone else's life. Do not be trapped by dogma - which is living with the results of other people's thinking. Do not let the noise of others' opinions drown out your inner voice. And most important, have the courage to follow your heart and intuition." Your ability to identify constraints will have a huge impact whether you can free yourself from self-limiting beliefs or not. The process of the identification of a limitation is necessary to recognise that those self- limiting beliefs only exist in your mind. Alleviating constraints can speed up the process of achievement as well as your attempts to start thinking big. Ask yourself what is holding you back to identify limitations and self-imposed limits.

Constraints could be the assumption that you need a university degree to make a career. There are a countless number of people around the world who made contributions in their small way to better human lives without going to college or a university. The lack of formal education is not as deadly as ignorance. And the cure to ignorance is not always formal education. Certificated learning even to the highest level is not the end of learning. To ensure one is not ignorant, one has to embark on continuous learning. Rather we could be restrained in the discovery, development, and deployment of our seed because of the mistake of comparing yourself to another; being intimidated by others' seed; living in isolation from those we perceive better than us.

Things That Hold People Back In Developing Their Seeds

There is no mystery to the discovery of your gift and subsequently developing it, whatever that may be. However, you often find that people hold back from developing their God-given seed. It is equally a tragedy for failing to discover your seed as it is to hold it back. You unlock your gifts, talent, skill and knowledge by just taking control of two things accessible to you and have precise control over it; the power to think and the power to act. When you consistently think through and work on the seed you have from your creator, you not only engage your potential, you also disengage your limits and the discouraging reasons to developing one's gifts. You begin in the right direction by focusing on reasons why you can. It all starts with the risk of believing more in yourself than in your limits. There will be times of crisis when logic tells you to abandon your pursuit to develop your gift. It is not a time to abandon your gift; it is a time to abandon your logic.

During crisis and adversity, remember that many things considered commonplace today were yesterday's miracles because someone refused to accept the logic of their time. I am not suggesting that you delude yourself into underestimating the destructive potential of the crisis. On the contrary, I am just stating that you can draw benefits from adversity by following the voice of God's spirit rather than logic and human understanding alone. Absolute logic without dependence on the Spirit of God, in looking for solutions is dangerous. Balancing logic and the direction of God's spirit is important but that notwithstanding there are things that possibly hold us back from developing our seeds.

Rejection

Rejection can lead you to feel like you're not good enough, since it often stems from criticism, from yourself or someone else. Use this criticism to learn how you can improve to succeed. Once you know what you have to develop, you can work on those areas and keep working at it again and again. If you keep learning and growing, you will succeed. A little rejection is inevitable, but if you're willing to keep trying, you will see both progress and results.

Having said all that, I must say that sometimes rejection could come from multiple sources. People are rejected by others sometimes because they are very different. When people cannot figure out who you are and what your purpose is all about there is the tendency for them to reject you. Individuals are denied access to certain opportunities merely because they are different from others and do not fit into the mold. Instead of celebrating diversity, and getting closer to know the person more they take the easiest and cynical route – rejection. You could have a negative perception of people until you get close to them and so whether it is in church, in the workplace or place of study, get to know people before you conclude on your opinion of them. Common sense is common, and yet not all people work with it at all times. It is just common sense to know that we are not the same and would never be same. The things that shape us into who we are, differ. Even in instances where you have two people experiencing the same thing the effect on the two would be different because of the two possible responses to those experiences and how that shapes them eventually. It is therefore not common sense to expect two people to be the same.

Also, insecurity from people because of the size of your seed and its potential to propel you to greatness, can trigger rejection from them. Although you may not be haughty because of what you carry on your life, you attract 'stick' from people. They first recognise what you have and devise a strategy to frustrate you by rejecting you. It is often the case that, the size of your seed determines your adversity, but it is an action emanating from a human proclivity to reject instead of celebrating others. It is a profoundly painful experience when those who see the seed in you, you don't see, try to kill it by rejecting you, when they should be supporting you to develop it for the benefit of humanity. They do this to get even with you, but no one ever got to the top and stayed at the top climbing on top of others. 'Success' obtained on the back of destroying others is a failure in disguise. Any form of 'success' that does not make the lives of others better is nothing but failure with a different name.

A chunk of my adult working life has been in the ministry, aside a few years I worked as a high school teacher. Although over the years I have utilised other skills I have, to offer paid services to organisations who need it. My observation over two decades in ministry is that there is rejection in ministry too. On one level you can experience rejection from the congregation in two ways; when you are different from the pastor who used to be in charge of the church before taking over and also when you are different from other pastors in the community, region, and nation where your ministry is based. On the second level there is also rejection from the clergy and Christians generally when there are allegations of impropriety of any form against you, whether verified or non-verified and in most cases when those reports of impropriety are found to be false, the damage has already been done. It is the fact that the same people who championed your persecution don't go back to everyone to say I was wrong because they are protecting their so-called reputations too. In most cases, they even hide the truth to this end. The rejection as a form of persecution is even more at its destructive best when the persecuted decides to leave the ministry altogether. In some cases, circulars are sent around churches to stay clear of that particular individual, or by customary default, members and clergy alike from those ministries cut off all associations with that particular person. You wonder whether those ministries are pursuing the building of some personal kingdoms or building the Kingdom of our God and of His Christ.

When you face rejection, you have to make a decision on the basis that; for whatever your assignment is, God found you worthy to carry it out for Him. You are answerable to Yahweh, and Him alone and the opinion of humankind go as far as their days on earth goes. It is the one who judges eternally whose opinion we must be concerned. They may even compare you to themselves and say because you haven't achieved at your age, what they accomplished at the age you are now, you're a failure or a nobody, but the truth is that God gave no two people the same assignment. And it is fatal for anyone to compare their achievements with others because what matters is whether such accomplishments fall within the perimeters of the job, if not it is no work done at all in the eyes of God. Keep your focus on your assignment or on whatever your life's endeavour is and work to fulfil it. If you want to be accepted and liked by everyone, you will die without your fulfilling your assignment.

Some people told me in the face God would never call a person like me and that I had no anointing for the work of the ministry. And in spite of their assessment, I have seen cancers healed, prophecies fulfilled, broken marriages healed, children born to women that doctors gave little or no chance of conception, elevation through strategic counsel, and other dramatic, stressful situations turn around in the lives of people in my ministry. I learned through these occurrences that what people perceive you to be and even make others believe about you doesn't matter. If you were to be responding to every barking dog you meet on the street, you would never reach your destination.

I had another experience, where people went as far as doing a background check on my parentage and concluded I wouldn't amount to anything much in life. What we must all seek is not the accolades of men and their acceptance but to fulfil our assignment here on earth to please God and make our world a better place for someone. If with all the celebrations of men, the accolades and honour accorded you, you fail to fulfil your assignment, you have failed. The irony of the situation is that it is also only Jehovah who can judge whether it is the task He's given you,

you are pursuing or your own to please men. The affirmations and condemnation in the court of human opinion are a great distraction to avoid at all cost.

Shake off rejection; it is not worth succumbing to it!

Rejection is also a tool of Satan through people against those who have a great assignment to do for God against him. It is a tool that Satan knows has immobilised a lot of people and therefore continue to use it.

Fear

Many people are held back in their lives because of fear. Fear of an outcome, fear of the unknown, fear of not being good enough, and fear of failing—we go through them all. You can pile fear on top of fear until eventually, you find it easier just to forget the whole idea and do something that makes you comfortable. Fear stems from our beliefs about ourselves, which is derived from our experiences and feedback from family and friends. If you have had a negative experience with something, then you may fear to experience that negative feeling all over again. If you feel you can't do something, you might take it in and be fearful that you really cannot do it. We typically harbour a fear of failure, fear of losing friends, fear of being disapproved or fear of not performing on the job, etc. One man said, "you can always tell the size of a man's identity by the scale of the problem it takes to discourage him." You need to remove these limiting beliefs and push past the fear.

Over two decades ago in one of the churches I pastored, I lost one of the members of my congregation, a young woman in the prime of her life. It was my first experience as a very young Pastor, to organise a funeral in the church. I had sleepless nights over my role, especially with the sermon and burial rites at the cemetery. It was a small town which had no prominent Pentecostal church but ours, at a time when people referred to Pentecostal Charismatic churches as 'mushroom churches' due to their nature of springing up everywhere 'overnight.' All eyes were on the church to see how well it would organise the funeral. I had to give a good impression of myself as a young contemporary pastor, considering that the town had funerals in the past organised by the old historic mission churches and were familiar with that.

I overcame it when I refused to let the fear of an anticipated daunting task immobilise me, but rode on the wave of fear to make sure I crossed all T's and dotted all I's. Sometimes the antidote to fear is to be well organised and ensure there is little room for any form of distraction, leaving nothing to chance for nasty surprises.

You can also put fear aside by using positive affirmations about yourself and consistently using positive self- talk to boost up your confidence level. It also helps to surround yourself with people who believe in you and in your abilities and push you forward to face your fears. There are times that what we fear never occurs in reality but only exists in our minds. The greatest limitations of our lives exist in our minds, and most of those limitations are a product of the fear we carry within us. To develop the seed God has placed in you, you would need to cast fear aside and push through. Whether it is the seed of God's anointing within, the seed of wisdom, business acumen and strategic envisioning, fear could let you hold back and not explore the potential of making use of the seed. The world needs to see that seed developed into a fully grown tree with seeds of its own to sustain others. Do not let fear hold you back.

Perceived Inabilities

God does not look at His people's weaknesses and past failures before making a decision to do great things through them. His presence consumes all weaknesses and adversity, and therefore in Him, all things are perfect (2 Corinthians 3:17). While we perceive our inabilities and hold back in developing the seed, God sees our potential to accomplish great things with our lives even in the adversity and limitations that confront us.

Gideon of the bible, had an inferiority complex which stemmed from his perceived inabilities and inadequacies in accomplishing anything great for the Lord. So even when the angel had addressed him the way God sees him, he was still recounting the failures of his times in connection to the lack of God's power. He asked the angel that if God was with him as he is saying then where are the miracles of old while they hide from their enemies? (Judges 6:13).

He had thought that the people of old who experienced the power of God in their time of adversity were more deserving than in his day. The image he had of himself caused him to remain restricted from advancing into his maximum potential. Before Gideon could walk in his destiny, God had to upgrade the image he had of himself and the image he had of God. Likewise, God will strengthen the picture you have of yourself, by revealing a deeper side of His character and ability to you, before you can fulfil His plan for your life. God's revelation of Himself to you will happen throughout the course of your life and ministry through designated times and seasons appointed by the Him. An example of this self-revelation of God to His people can be seen in the life of Abraham as earlier discussed in this chapter. Over a period of twenty-five years, the Lord on several occasions visited Abraham to build into him a stronger image of his ability. From the time God called Abraham out in Genesis 12, through to the fulfilment of Isaac's birth, the Lord chose particular seasons to visit Abraham to strengthen the image he had of God. It was to let Abraham believe that if He was with God, then his perceived inabilities didn't count because it was no more of his strength but God's. Although Abraham is one of the patriarchs of faith, he often struggled with the idea of the promise God made to him.

> *"I will make you a great nation; I will bless*
> *you and make your name great"*
> *Genesis 12:2.*

The Lord had to build into Abraham's heart and mind an image of what the Lord was able to do through him.

He did this by replacing old thought patterns, mental images and imaginations with new ones. Likewise, the Lord desires to replace old mentalities with new ones too, to fulfil His blue-print for your life. It is probable that if Peter had not held the hand of the lame beggar to prop him up, he would not have been healed.

He rated his inability above the power of God.

> *"And he took him by the right*
> *hand and lifted him up, and*
> *immediately his feet and ankle*
> *bones received strength."*
> *(Acts 3:7)*

Sometimes we know that we cannot do something because we tried or have in our own way assessed our capabilities, and sometimes we had tried to do something before and failed. For instance, if you have never tried swimming before, then taking on the challenge of swimming across a lake may seem unrealistic. On the other hand, if you had sought to swim across the lake before and failed, then you may hold the belief that you just cannot do it. On the other hand, if you know someone who is good at it and done it before encouraging you to do it as you have the stamina and required technique based on his observation, you may want to try. That is what God does in our lives, He let us know we can make it, because he made the lake and made us too.

Fortunately for us, our perceived inability is something that everyone can push past. With enough effort, you can learn almost anything you set your mind to and accomplish it. You just have to find the information or help and start learning and practicing. For example, you can take piano lessons, even if you need to start from an absolute beginner class. Eventually, you will move on to intermediate and advanced levels, and soon you could be playing at a professional level. Even at the professional level, you would have to keep practicing till you are able to maintain your performance at a certain peak of excellence. It is at this point that it is evident you're distinguished and set apart from other professionals in the field. You just have to start small and keep at it. The temptation is that when you do not push past your perceived inabilities, you will settle into your comfort zone. Do not let your comfort zone hold you back from taking risks, reaching your potential, breaking your limits and experiencing success. The more you push through your comfort zone, the larger it will become. Soon it will come much more naturally and easily to do things that move you toward your dreams.

It's time for a check-up. Just as it is important to have periodic physical check-ups, we need to have spiritual check-ups on a regular basis. We need to check and see if we are paying enough attention to the seeds in our life and are producing the right expected kind of fruits. That sort of check–up discussed here takes diligent work. Being lazy may have grave consequences to developing your seed. Do not risk your future with the obstructive trends or undesirable pursuits. Be diligent in cultivating the seed God has placed in you for great accomplishment. Adversity and afflictions with its limitations may arise upon us, but we are still more than able to get through it with the seed we have all received. The apostles, Peter and John recognised what they had and knew what they had within was not what the disabled beggar expected but they also knew it was what he needed to break his limitations. Can you imagine a situation where the apostles themselves didn't know what they had as in the power of God? It would have been a missed opportunity to demonstrate that ordinary person, and for that matter, everyone has a seed in him given by God for the days of adversity. By that demonstration, it was also equally a message for the disabled beggar to recognise that his place was not the Beautiful gate where he sat daily begging for alms. And that somehow he had what it takes from within to be better placed in life. In one way it was also to say to the disabled beggar that, 'yes people would give you from their toil, but there's nothing like being able to do it for yourself.' It was a way to say; it is time to change paradigms, it is time to grow up. It is the time to recognise the seed within.

CHAPTER FOUR

THE FRUIT: GROWING IN ADVERSITY

The Apostles Peter and John asking the disabled beggar to look at them in expectation was also to assist him to change paradigms. It was to shift in paradigms from dependency to recognising the treasure of a seed that lies within. They did this by demonstrating they had something with the capability of transforming a life no matter the background, past experiences and current circumstances of adversities and limitations. The result of that experience or better still, what the Apostles wanted to achieve was to assist the beggar to grow on the back of his own experiences.

In other words, they used his experience as a learning curve for him to grow in his understanding. Aside from the Apostles using that meeting with the disabled beggar at the beautiful gate to assist him to shift paradigms, what this encounter also teaches us is that every experience both positive and negative gives us the opportunity to grow. In every situation of adversity, there is an equal opportunity for growth in various areas of life. We measure growth by the fruits you produce as a result of the experience. It is true that difficult situations either make you bitter or better. The resulting attitude, character, lifestyle you develop from those experiences is what defines you as a person. So we would largely in this chapter be discussing fruits but as a product of the growth process that takes place in our lives, consequent to the adversities and limitations that confront us.

The Christian life is all about knowing God and His Son Jesus Christ and bearing fruit. As believers, we have been empowered to be fruitful, multiply, replenish the earth, and dominate it (Genesis 1:28), but there are forces in life that have been designed to limit us from walking into the plan and purposes of God for our lives. Both spiritually and physically God's desire for us is to be able to bear fruit. Jesus stated that those that call themselves His disciples and would recognise them as such are those that bear fruit (John 15:8). Bearing fruit is very important as it connects us to a living God, considering that God through Jesus Christ lives in us. Living organisms have an innate propensity to produce after their kind, even when subjected to harsh environmental factors. That is to say that God gave the command to bear fruit, there was no attention paid to the environmental factors as a threat. The reason is that the life force in that seed is enormous and unstoppable. The multiple transitions of the life-force in a seed that enables it to thrive, grow and bear fruit are itself progress.

God's desire is for you and I make to steady progress, we are not designed to be contained or restricted by anything. Each one of us is expected to use the gift for us to have an impact on our lives and the lives of others. We should not make an excuse for our limitations in God's quest for us to bear fruits. Whatever the situation is, we can bear fruit. It is God's command for us to bear fruit that is why we cannot limit ourselves like the lame man at the beautiful gate and at the same time proclaim ourselves God's children. He sat at a gate where people coming through that gate, in their own way were making progress with their lives, and yet he was at the gate begging for alms making a living from their sympathies. From the sort of interaction that the Apostles had with the disabled beggar, it was evident the kind of life he had at that moment in time was not the will of God for him. A life where he depended on others was not a life of fruit bearing or progress. The message to the disabled beggar was clear; he was meant to live a more fruitful and productive life.

There is a similar narrative about a time when God's people were in bondage as slaves in Egypt. Their state of being slaves and circumstances did not stop them from engaging in the processes of human reproduction.

To the extent that the scriptures note that the more they were afflicted by their slave masters the more, they grew (Exodus 1:12). Although the plan was to wear them out completely, that plan backfired on the slave masters. There was something within that could not be restricted or diminished by adversity and human-induced limitations placed on them by their slave masters. At some point, they even complained when Moses arrived with a mission to negotiate their release from servitude because their slave masters subjected them to more hardship. Their slave masters abhorred the thought of their release from bondage since they represented a cheap and efficient labour force used in building the Egyptian economy. They worked so hard in the most horrible and torturous conditions but were not paid for work done.

Their impromptu release meant a sudden decline in the Egyptian economy because not even the mature modern economies of our day can deal with the shocks to losing 600,000 people of its productive and active workforce all at once without the prospects of an immediate replacement. All this meant that it was impossible for the Egyptians to let them go. And since Moses was the one who had given them the idea of a possible release they increased their workload so the people would blame Moses and rebel against any such idea of leaving. It is an enigma that sometimes people make you feel worthless and yet when you walk out on them, they feel the pain and wish you had not left. The bottom line is that, you were useful to them but they won't let you know whilst you were with them for fear that would increase your sense of worth and rebellion could follow. The strategy of increasing their workload was to make the whole process even harder for Moses because now, it would not just be the Egyptians who are refusing the release of God's people, but God's people are fighting the whole idea because of the suffering at the hands of the Egyptians. The bottom line is that their taskmasters were fearful that through that process of biological reproduction they might one day outnumber them and join with their enemies to rebel and therefore passed a decree to kill all males.

It was a less thought through action born out of desperation. To analyse it from their perspective, if they killed all male-born, they were directly disinheriting God's people because they operated a patriarchal system. That would be equally as destroying the fabric of their society because the men represented economics, industry, governance, development, and politics. However, what they failed to perceive was that killing all Israeli males meant starving Egypt some of the very things they purposed to destroy in the future society of God's people - the economics, industry and infrastructural development.

Another thing that precipitated the treatment from the Egyptians slave masters was the fear that if they didn't physically wear them out, they could come together with their enemies to turn on them, and make them, the owners of the land, subjects. The key to the turn-around of the difficulties of God's people was that of being fruitful and increasing in number. The strategy God adopted for His people in bondage holds true for us that, our way of overcoming adversity and breaking limitations is to be fruitful. The best way to answer your critics is to continue to make progress with your endeavours and bear fruit. As you increase and become bigger, sometimes the very people who criticised, maligned and undermined you, have no choice than to change the stories and identify with you.

When you do a proper exegesis of Isaiah 10:27 it gives a meaning that is entirely different in the way that text has been over spiritualised because of the use of the word anointing. The anointing refers to a spiritual empowerment to accomplish unusual things possibly above a person's natural capabilities. Within the context of Scripture, the 'yoke', is an implement used to control animals in the field of land cultivation and 'anointing', as the pouring of oil, representing fat from the animal as symbols that were commonplace and well understood at the time. The implied figure is that of a bullock which grows so fat that the yoke will no longer go around its neck, as people are stronger through productivity, and fruitful function-ability to assert their freedom from adversities and limitations. When you grow, whether it is economic, mentally, socially, or spiritually certain restrictions lose their hold on you along the way as part of that process of expansion.

Reminiscent of the life of the disabled beggar is life, where those who should be on their feet are carried or those who should be in charge are under supervision. In the same way, the Apostles tried to bring the disabled beggar to a particular understanding that growth was the key to health, freedom and new life for him, it was a little act of 'look at us' and saying 'silver and gold we do not have' it was his expectation based on his experience of begging, that help him shift paradigms. They educated him, and therefore he grew as his reaction to give his hand to these men to lift him up says it all. Mentally he had shifted from dependency to self-dependency.

Sometimes when people are not able to get enough from their work, they may think that taking on an extra job or working extra harder may be the solution to their financial insufficiency, but the answer may lie in growing professionally to move up the career ladder. The growth may occur as a consequence of continuous education, skill training, or even changing your workplace mentor. What sometimes you need to realise in your life isthat with every growth some limitations are broken off as a matter of course. Certain happenings in your life may seem to be beyond your strength if you intend to tackle them directly. However, as you concentrate on growth and increase in areas of your life, generally you would in that process be breaking those limitations you have in your life. For instance, if you have massive debts that seem insurmountable to clear. You may not be creditworthy to obtain a loan to consolidate all debts together to pay them off, but you could take up classes on finance management, so you know how to handle money better. Or you could also take up a skills training to move up the career ladder if not for a complete career change, to earn more to manage the payment of the debts. Otherwise, it would not matter the amount of money you make because there is debt - limitations you are still far away from personal financial freedom. Like the disabled beggar, the disability which was a huge weakness at the time had thwarted his ability to earn a decent living through the work of his hands. He knew quite well and how relevant it was to work and was also willing to work to fend for himself but because of his disability, he could not do it.

It was this that the Apostles Peter and John picked up from a quick glance at him, knew that giving him money would not solve the problem that brought him to the beautiful gate in the first place. Whatever amount they gave him would not have ever solved his problem. They, therefore, gave him what would solve his problem forever. Like the old Chinese adage 'Give a man a fish, and you have fed him once. Teach him how to fish, and you have fed him for a lifetime.' This principle regarding fishing implies that the ability to work is of greater benefit than a one-off handout or it is better to know how to help yourself than to beg from others.

God did not create and designate to anyone a life of begging or endless suffering, although I believe suffering is part of the human life and sometimes unavoidable as it combines with other human occurrences to spurn growth in us. Late in the year 2006 in prayer, my wife and I kept receiving revelations about a child of a relative who had died, and we were part of a burial procession. The coffin was white, with white roses and lilies draped on it, in a hearse to the cemetery. We prayed intensively about it for a couple of months until we no longer saw it again or sensed it was going to happen.

The long and short of the story is that we lost our son in January the following year and it happened that the funeral home we contacted to undertake the burial used the same white coffin, and draped it with white roses and lilies as we saw in those revelations a couple of months before. It was a harrowing experience, but I can tell you there is a lot I learned from that experience through asking questions and seeking answers to what had happened. Why we prayed about it for so long and yet it happened? Why didn't we know it was our son specifically who was going to pass away? And also the fact that before my son was born, we haven't as yet decided on the name to give him at birth till one day while lying down, the Lord told me to call him Emmanuel, which meant 'God with us.' So did God wanted us to know He was with us when all was said and done? I started putting all these pieces together to make sense of the whole experience. In the end, we grew in our understanding of the ways of God, and our place with Him, and also of spiritual warfare.

It is the wish of God that all people on earth will live happily in health and prosperity; "Beloved, I pray that you may prosper in all things and be in health, just as your soul prospers." (3 John 1:2). That is why God said in Genesis that the firmament of the heavens which means the space of heavens has enough room to accommodate everyone on earth with enough resources for everyone to exploit and to express one's purpose and to fulfil destiny. Many do not bear fruit because they consider the cost of that process too high. Would you bear the cost to bear fruit?

The Cost Of Growth

The Apostles John and Peter offered to the disabled beggar what they had which they have received from Christ. Through our analysis with the apostle's encounter with the disabled beggar, the beggar had something within that should make his life better. It was for that reason they requested he focused on them to change his mental picture of self-indulging and self-limiting beliefs and see through them what he could also be. It is time to stress that the apostles had paid the price to have what they had and to have developed it to the point that they were so sure they could deliver at that moment in time when they met the disabled beggar.

Do not forget that some of these disciple's including these who met the disabled beggar had left their jobs and businesses to follow Christ in the hope of a better future. There were even times they didn't know what to eat or where to sleep. And yet for what they perceived, they stood to benefit they stuck with Jesus through good and bad times, through times of rebuke and commendation from Jesus till the time they took over the ministry Jesus left behind.

To give this brief background of the Apostles about what the Apostle Peter referred to as 'such as we have, we give,' there is an amount of work or personal sacrifices needed to bring about the fruit. We have already discussed the fact that bearing fruit in itself involves the process of growth. It is the growth that necessitates bearing fruit and growth requires sacrifices. That is God's expectation from His perspective. An example of this point of view can be seen from the Prophet's Isaiah' prophesy to Israel. In Chapter 54:1-4;

> *"Sing, O barren, You who have not borne! Break forth into singing, and cry aloud, You who have not labored with child! For more are the children of the desolate Than the children of the married woman," says the Lord. "Enlarge the place of your tent, And let them stretch out the curtains of your dwellings; Do not spare; Lengthen your cords, And strengthen your stakes. For you shall expand to the right and to the left, And your descendants will inherit the nations, And make the desolate cities inhabited. "Do not fear, for you will not be ashamed; Neither be disgraced, for you will not be put to shame; For you will forget the shame of your youth, And will not remember the reproach of your widowhood anymore".*

The message of the scripture above was an announcement of the vast provision of vicarious atonement through the Suffering Servant; the prophet announces the following blessings: the expansion of Israel, the blessings of safety and peace, and the portion of righteousness. The entire chapter anticipates the salvation and restoration of Israel, it began in part at the reinstatement of the exiles from Babylon in 536 B.C. in the future, for as this chapter unfolded, it was clear that return did not exhaust the promises.

An analysis of the scripture with the symbolisms used there and what that teaches us about our responsibility and sacrifices, needed to bring about growth with culminates in bearing fruit. The promised significant provision was coming in the form of human biological reproduction and therefore to accommodate the number of children to be given to the people there was need to enlarge the place of their tent. In other words, there was going to be an increase in resources for prestige, honour, and productivity but before that happens preparations must be set to make it happen. The essence of prophecy was with regards to being able to contain the anticipated increase. Using the same symbolism to explain, because they had no children they lived in tents, with sizes that could only accommodate a couple but with the arrival of new additions to the families they needed of a necessity to make more room. In other words, they needed to build their capacity to handle what was coming their way as a blessing. They needed to grow their spaces to be able to contain more. As exciting as this promise sounds, there was an element of personal responsibility.

The responsibility to make the personal sacrifices required to enlarge the tent of their dwelling to make room for the new arrivals.

That responsibility lies on every individual who wants to grow to bear fruit. It is a responsibility no one would carry except the one with the commitment and expectation to bear fruit. The commitment to grow is true for almost every area of life's endeavour, financially, mentally, education, family life, and relationships. I remember when I started my MBA program, I had difficulties in understanding some of the basic concepts and terminologies used in the business world. I had only studied business up to the A' levels most of which were self-taught and through private tuition for my exams. I did this while I was still training to be a teacher full time. Combining the two was extremely difficult but I was determined to make the most of my time while I was still young. I pursued a Bachelors in Theology and Religions a couple of years after that, so that was about everything I had learned about business up to that point. So being on an MBA program was challenging and catching up with others who had Bachelors in business related programs and made contributions during lectures was intimidating. However, I realised if I wanted to do well and stop embarrassing myself at group discussions and preparations for group presentations, I had to do extra work. I committed myself to doing that extra work until I completed the program successfully. That program has opened doors for me and granted me access to places, but before that could happen, I had to put in the necessary work.

So it is with the spiritual, whatever the spiritual entanglements you find yourself, God has given you the weapons to deal with it. It is time to make the personal sacrifices to break from the bondage to bear fruit. You must tackle spiritual matters spiritually and physical matter physically. You should not hope that things will be well just for the sake of it. Things do not just happen; nothing in this world happens by chance. Certain sacrifices have to be made to make progress or see growth which is necessary for bearing fruit. We have been given spiritual weapons to deal with spiritual things, where confronting other spirit entities are involved. These weapons are deployed mainly through the agency of prayer. You need to rise and pray, so that which God has said about your life will come to pass or use the weapons of spiritual warfare through the agency of prayer to break limitations in your life. Prayer is also critical for sustenance through adversity as it draws the comforting and strengthening presence of God. In the book of 1Kings 18, when Elijah told King Ahab that there would be an abundance of rain, Elijah did not sleep, he put behind him the comfort of staying in his home and climbed a mountain and sat on the undergrowth of the mountain floor in prayer.

As he prayed, in the process he sent his servant about seven different times to check for signs of rain bearing cloud but he found none. The report did not discourage him persisting in his endeavour. He endured until the cloud started to form and eventually it rained heavily breaking the cycle of three and half years of drought.

Elijah trusted God in what he had said and prayed about it till it happened. You also need to cultivate the habit of waiting upon God through the agency of prayer to see His workings in your life. You need to have a regular and consistent time to fast and pray for others and yourself. There is no reason why you would not receive from him what it takes to overcome your adversity and break every limit on your life. God will surely glorify Himself as you do it, as He did for Elijah and the lame man as we examine that in detail in the next chapter. To this end, James 5:17 says, 'Elijah was a man with a nature like ours, and he earnestly prayed that it would not rain, and it did not rain on the land for three years and six months.' It is another way of saying that if Elijah was able to petition the heavens to bring about down rain, then we are also capable and would get the same results as he did if we also pray earnestly.

The key thing in these examples as from Elijah and the disabled beggar was that they had to look beyond themselves for solutions. They had to shift paradigms to realise in concrete terms what it is they sought after. When the lame man asked for alms from Peter and John, they told him "look at us," he had to shift his attention from himself for that moment in time to the possibility to see something new beyond the familiar. His familiar, was self-defeat and lost hope.

Again, it does require work to live our lives worthy of the high calling of Christ. It takes effort, discipline, and commitment to bear the fruit of righteousness. In other words, to be more like Christ in every way. God's ultimate aim is for us to reach the same level of spiritual maturity and stature as Christ. Christian growth is about applying principles from God's word that will empower you, and provide tools with which to overcome adversity. Every individual would once upon a time would have to face adversity, and break limits for the greater expression of what our Creator has made us to be. Thus creating room for you to focus and seek more of Christ into your life and strive to be like Him. There was a crusade held in Uganda by some missionaries some years ago. During the gospel crusade, the preacher spoke about Jesus' death and resurrection. One of the attendees of the crusade told one of the missionaries that he knew the burial place of Jesus and he has not risen to heaven as alluded. The preacher wanted to know more about this Jesus. The discussion led them to the grave of the 'Jesus' they have been discussing.

To the discovery of the missionary, the person whose grave they went to was also a missionary. The astonishing testimony about the former minister was that he lived like Christ about whom the missionaries preached. The individuals in the town saw Christ in him, and they saw him as Christ. His entire life was about being like Christ in every way he possibly could. Certainly, the grave they visited was not that of the historical Christ of the Bible this person at the crusade had led the missionary to, because Jesus Christ rose from the dead and sits on the right-hand side of God the Father. What is intriguing about this story is that we could aspire to make our lives all about Christ and be like him, no matter what the circumstances of our lives dictate. Whether it's during the time of adversity, dealing with some limitations or at a terrible time of our lives. We can grow to be more like our saviour Jesus Christ. In that way, we would be able to live a life that others may emulate. Paul, the Apostle, did the same when he urged his followers to imitate him as he imitates Christ. "Imitate me, just as I also imitate Christ" (1 Corinthians 11:1). It is entirely possible to keep growing in the Lord, living lives that will let people see Jesus in us. People should be able to have the desire to turn over their lives to Christ when they see you, wanting to be like you. We need to come to a place where our lives are like that of Christ. We should be able to live our lives as Christ lived His.

There is no question whatsoever that, growth is only possible we make necessary sacrifices and work hard. We could achieve a likeness to Christ in all we do. We should be able to live a life of Christ-likeness everywhere we find ourselves. Our lives of righteousness and right-living should not only be limited to coming to the house of God. We should be able to demonstrate the Christ in us in our workplaces, homes, in the shopping mall, in the car park, when happy or angry or when provoked. It is through your lifestyle that people will know you.

In addition to the areas of our lives needing growth, we cannot conclude this section without making mention of growth of godly character within the broader concept of the cost to pay for growth in our lives which is necessary for fruit. In ancient and modern times, people have used "fruit" to mean results, products, outcomes, accomplishments, and achievements. An employee must be productive, obtaining results with tasks assigned by the employer to be worthy of his or her wages. They must work hard, work fast and work smart to get jobs done and done right effectively and efficiently. The same way, the Bible at times likens people to fruit trees or grapevines and portrays God as the owner of the orchards and vineyards. The fruit we are supposed to bear is the character traits we show in different situations. The Master knows our nature by our spiritual fruits, just as a tree is identified by its fruit whether for good or bad reasons.

> *"...A good tree cannot bear bad fruit, nor can a bad tree bear good fruit. Every tree that does not bear good fruit is cut down and thrown into the fire. Therefore by their fruits you will know them."* (Matthew 7:18-20)

It is through the fruit you bear you will be defined as a person, as our character defines us. Significant accomplishments without a godly character are like building a house without reinforcement to hold it all up and keep it standing for a long time. A godly character with accomplishment even makes it greater as many people would take inspiration from it and would be proud to associate with it.

There are three phrases within the verse of scripture above that we need to take note of;

Every Tree Bears Fruit Of Its Kind.

Every tree is supposed to produce after its kind according to the natural order of things. What it means is that a mango tree cannot bear orange fruits and vice versa. It is virtually impossible for it to be otherwise. The health of the tree determines the health of its fruit, the ground on which the tree stand and the availability of nutrients determine how well the tree would do. It is the presence of the Holy Spirit, that makes one becomes spiritually alive, beginning a new life. God's Spirit is like the life-giving sap that flows up the trunk of a tree to all its branches so they can yield fruit. Therefore, if you are born of the Spirit, then you must have fruits originating from the Spirit of God. It cannot be otherwise in the same way it is in a tree. There are many places in scripture where God portrays His people as flourishing fruit trees (Jeremiah 17:7-8; compare Psalms 1:3). The background to this sort of analogy has always been that he has been their source of life enabling them to produce the supply of the necessary soil nutrients. And so it is almost a non- negotiable fact that once planted in God, you would bear fruit that should identify you with Him as the source or the grounds. It is, therefore, a limitation for people in the body of Christ to refuse to bear fruits that identify with Christ and glorify Him.

Unfortunately, the disabled beggar at the Beautiful Gate's limitation prevented him from bearing fruit socio- economically and needed that to be broken to be fruitful in those areas of his life he was limited. If you scrutinize the process of seed germination, in instances where the seed has a hard seed shell or husk the shell softens by the conditions of the soil in which it stands, and then the new life force within the seed pushes out of its enclosure to grow. So, to bear fruit, something has to die or be broken in the first instance to make way for the new life. As believers in Christ, we do not produce this fruit automatically; it's not natural, we produce it because of our relationship with Christ, and He's the ground on which we stand. That is to say that He has His way with us while we have yielded our lives to Him making an effort daily to be more like Him in every way. As we understand the kind of fruit that we ought to bear in our lives, we keep in mind that it takes some effort and sacrifice on our part. The sacrifice and effort are the cost we have to pay for growth. As anyone invites Jesus into their lives, and begin to submit to Him as the Lord of their lives, through obedience, they start to look more like Him and less like their natural self – the Adamic nature. Over time through your acquaintance with the Lord, there ought to be a noticeable shift in the direction of your life toward godliness and exhibiting a godly character.

The Quality Of The Fruit Is Determined By The Quality Of The Tree.

The properties of a tree are natural to its unique chemical composition and structure. Its properties are also passed on to its fruits, whose seeds are supposed to produce trees and then fruits of its kind in that cycle. The process goes a long way to explain the fact that if the fruit is sweet, it is an indication of the chemical properties of the tree from which the fruit comes. The process of reproduction of trees teaches us a lesson that whatever fruits we are bearing is an indication of the source of which we are connected to and operate. Thus what we produce as outcomes in our lives as being fruitful or otherwise, is a consequence of the source from which we draw. If that is the case, then we should make sure to be grafted to the right kind of tree to produce the right kind of fruit. Most of the time you may do something wrong, and you later realise what you have done, it is a check of dis-alignment in your heart as you may be grafting a bad fruit on a good tree. In that way, it is a warning light of a mismatch and our conscience brings it to our attention that way.

The Fruit Is An Indicator Of The Fruitfulness Of The Tree

> "23 Keep your heart with all diligence,
> For out of it spring the issues of life."
> (Proverbs 4:23).

As we have already discussed in the previous section, what we do on a daily basis is an indicator of what is within us and what is within us determines who we are. So a person who consistently shows compassion, for instance, is a compassionate person. One of the important fruit a believer can bear is compassion. Compassion has a price tag if anyone desires that kind of fruit. Growth is the requirement for the fruit of compassion. The Apostles Peter and John had it in abundance. It was compassion that made them stop by the disabled beggar, not an interest to show off the power of God. It does not come as a surprise that Peter writes; "Finally, all of you be of one mind, having compassion for one another; love as brothers, be tenderhearted, be courteous" (1Peter 3:8).

Compassion is a sympathetic consciousness of others distresses together with the desire to alleviate it. When a distressful situation touches your heart without the desire to do something about it, is not compassion. Compassion goes beyond feeling pity about someone's situation to taking steps to assist in any way you can to either make it bearable if it is beyond redemption. It was compassion that moved Jesus Christ to heal their sick when He saw the crowd as having no one to care for them and help those that had infirmities (Matthew 14:14). Compassion always accompanies zeal or the willingness to help to solve the problem as demonstrated by Jesus in His ministry and by Apostles Peter and John when they met the disabled beggar. When you are not moved to the extent of acting whether direct or indirect, then it is just sympathy without action. Sometimes, people in need approach other individuals who are in a position to help, but they do not help, rather they rationalise their response not to support to feel good but deep within realise they haven't done the right thing. Before one starts thinking of compassion as a gift from God to particular people and not everyone has what it takes to be compassionate to people in their time of need, we need to remember what we discussed in the previous section that the source or the tree determines the fruit. Therefore, if we are Christs and have the Holy Spirit in us then we are supposed to be compassionate too.

However, some people do things according to their reasoning and understanding even when they are touched to respond with compassion to another's plight. When others are in need, and you can help, think but help.

Most people have lost compassion in their hearts towards people no matter the circumstances, and it is because of the individualistic lifestyle we have developed over time, we have lost value for humanity. It is sad to say that people would put their career, business, money, and other material possessions above the lives of humans so long as it serves their purpose. One of the things Jesus exhibited in His life, was the value He placed on people.

Also, we should not also judge people before we help them as we may not understand everything about them or their situation by our presumption. We may be wrong. We should reserve the right to judge to God. I read a story many years ago, the source I don't remember, where a man was traveling with his children on a bus. The kids were misbehaving while they were on the bus, walking on the seat and making noise disturbing the peace of other travellers. The situation was embarrassing to those who had children with them who were relatively calm. It was also very annoying that most of the passengers on the bus thought the father of the children should be considerate enough to call his children to order because they were in a public space. They wondered why the man had remained adamant about calling his children to order.

One of the passengers approached the man to confront him about his lack of responsibility as a parent to control his kids on a public transport. The man told him the children had just witnessed the passing away of their mother in the hospital and he believes it is the children's way of venting their anger, pain, and frustration, hence the unruly behaviour. Immediately, the passenger received the news he apologised to the man, commiserated with him and left him alone. When the Enquirer took his seat, he whispered the news to others in the bus. Although the children did not stop the unruly behaviour entirely on the bus the other passengers with whom they were traveling stopped complaining and rather had compassion on the kids asking how they could be of help in any way they could. Sometimes when you do not understand an occurrence or even a situation someone finds themselves, you may pass wrong judgment. Therefore, you do not need to understand everything about a person before you offer help, just help.

Jesus never underestimated the value of people he came across, and neither did His disciples. If they did, then the disabled beggar wouldn't have received the kind of attention the Apostles gave him. Refusing to look down on the beggar was a way of showing the nature of Christ in them. If you indeed have Christ in you, you should not be self-centred but rather always be thinking about how to help and make life better for others. We have an innate satisfaction when we show concern for others' welfare and take steps to help them in ways we can. Value people and make people your priority in all your dealings. People who typically value material things over humans regret it when they find themselves in situations needing the compassion of others to support them. We are unable to exhibit the same compassion as Christ did because of greed, self- gratification and the high value we place on material things to the disadvantage of humans. We have a responsibility as believers to live as Christ did if indeed we are connected to Him as a branch. There must be fruits to identify Him as our source.

Finally, in a summary to this chapter, the Apostles made it a point to ask the disabled beggar to look at them, with the intention of shifting his attention from the negative mental images of himself in the present, and in the future which gave rise to, his begging for alms. As discussed earlier, they needed to let him develop new mental images of health, prosperity, and independence as a preparation to receive what he needed other than the alms. The limitation was the paralysis which was the underlying cause of his inability to work and earn a living like everyone else. In the end, as he obeyed their instruction they gave him what he had which was the fruit of their years of walking with Christ and the promise of the Holy Spirit. They didn't have what the disabled beggar asked for but had even more of exactly what he needed, for which they gave in the name of Jesus Christ of Nazareth.

CHAPTER FIVE

IN THE NAME OF JESUS

The disabled beggar focused on them in expectation to receive, since what the Apostles had from Christ through the Holy Spirit on Pentecost could only be delivered to its maximum potential in the name of Jesus. The reason being that it is the name of Jesus is recognisable in both the earthly and spiritual realm. We would remind ourselves as in previous chapters, to analyse this part of the story from three different perspectives; the view to the disabled beggar, the point of view of the Apostles Peter and John, and from the perspective of someone reading the entire narrative. The focus as a reminder is to draw principles, examples, and inspiration for the story on how to deal with adversity and break limits on our lives. It is a common sight to see and hear believers praying in the name of Jesus as did the Apostles Peter and John. However, the question is what is the name?

In ancient Israel, names were designed to distinguish objects and initially expressed the distinct impressions that object made upon one or the special relations in which they stood to the person. So for instance in Genesis 2:19, God brought the animals to Adam and from the impression they made on him he assigned names to them. It was also the same when God presented Adam with the woman, he looked at the woman, and said 'this is the bone of my bones and flesh of my flesh, she shall be called Eve' (Genesis 2:23). Again, in some sense, a name to the Israelite was a sign of something entirely outward, and it is for this reason that names were rarely hereditary in Hebrew societies at the time.

Names generally within the context of Hebrew society expressed some personal characteristic, some incident connected with the birth as in the case of Jabez (1 Chronicles 4:9-10), some hope or wish or prayer of the parent. Also, there were names given based on an event considered necessary, a chance word, a pious or hopeful expression by the mother and even a well- omened word was seized and attached to a new born. There were times newborns were named based on their time of birth such as Zerubbabel which means 'born in Babylon' or Hodesh which means 'new moon.' There were also times when names given initially at birth are changed for a new one, or a new one is added. For example, Abram's name was changed to 'Abraham' when God renewed His covenant with him; Jacob the 'supplanter' became 'Israel.' Names in Hebrew custom and tradition is sometimes used to signify the collected attributes or characteristics of the object or person so named. And this is in particular reference to divine names, it indicated how God reveals Himself and His attributes to humankind in a way they could understand and relate to him.

Some names were prophetically assigned such as the name of Jesus, the saviour (Luke 1:31). He also received the name, Christ, as having been consecrated by His baptism and the descent of the Holy Spirit as our Prophet, Priest, and King. To understand the whole mystery of the power that exists in Jesus' name is to understand who this man who once walked the earth but now seated at the right hand of God is. Jesus had a unique birth unlike all other children by natural reproduction. He was conceived by the Holy Spirit of the Virgin Mary, giving us the indication that He was God incarnate if we critically examine the gospels and especially the Gospel according to St John, where John says '...was with God' and '..was God...' and '...became flesh..' (John 1:1-14). He was the promised 'Lamb of God' and 'the lamb led to the slaughter' meant to pay for the sins of the human kind John 1:29; Isaiah 53:7). Considering that as a result of sin, man had been far removed and separated from God

– spiritually dead. The death which God had spoken to Adam and Eve was to happen should they disobey and make a wrong choice of the fruit trees in the garden at the time. The initiation and promulgation of the over 615 laws designated as the law of Moses were an interim measure meant to keep humankind in right standing with God, but that failed as God knew and foretold of His ultimate plan to offer His son. And so it became necessary that someone had to be sent when the time was just right for God through His son, to die for human kind. So that man through the sacrifices of His son could be reconciled back to God. On his birth and life, He was sinless though encompassed about with sin, afflicted with error and had frailty common to all other humans. Although He was sinless, He had the keenest sensitivity to sin; he was never conscious of sin in himself until the sin of the world was laid on him on the cross at Calvary. He had no sin and therefore never confessed sin (1 John 3:5). In His death, the sufferings of Christ are entirely different from those of any other human being.

The agony in the garden and the sweat that became like drops of blood were the results not merely of extreme mental and physical anguish on the human plane but were occasioned by the sinless soul of the Son of God coming into contact with the weight of the world's sin. The sufferings of Calvary are more than the excruciating pain of crucifixion or body-racking thirst, but coming into contact with sin and enduring for that moment the wrath of God. In addition to the above, Christ's miraculous resurrection was the shattering of history by a creative act of Jehovah, His Father through the resurrection of Christ. God was doing something in comparative nature to the process of creation and creation itself. His resurrection is a great experienced reality that makes clear all the other facts of the person and work of Christ. It is in the resurrection of Christ that He fulfilled His incipient announcement of the purpose of His coming into the world, 'I came that they might have life and might have it abundantly' (John 10:10). It is through these qualifications which he earned in the sight of God that has made it possible for him to represent us in God's presence.

So that when we approach the Father in His name, we are given unhindered access to Him. The name Jesus granted access to God the Father and recognised in the Kingdom of Darkness. At the mention of the name of Jesus, every knee in heaven, on earth and under the earth bows and every tongue on earth, under the earth and in heaven confess that he is Lord (Philippians 2:10). By way of explanation, Jesus authority over all things and rules over all (Ephesians 1:21). The eternal life of God in Him and the power in His name which He obtained through His suffering on the cross, His death, and His Resurrection, believers have access to corridors of spiritual authority with power.

Practical evidence exists for those exposed to such testimonies including myself that those who have rested their faith in a crucified and risen Redeemer have experienced the regenerating touch of God upon their lives. No change is as remarkable as the one that takes place in the person who begins to have faith in Jesus Christ. Through the divine arrangement, He is looking for individuals who are Kingdom minded; individuals who are willing to do things which may not be convenient for them but for the benefit of His Kingdom that He could work mighty things through them. Believers who understand and recognise this call to greater works have received the full package of Christ in His name to that effect. The name of Jesus carries authority, but ignorance of the power in the name and its efficacy is robbing many of God's blessings and fulfilment. The fact that the name of Jesus has become a cliché, a jargon as part of Christian prayer, it has lost the faith with which it needs to be said by the believer. The ignorance of the power in the name of Jesus in my estimation is the reason why the enemy has kept people in the dark about it, unknown to many believers. The enemy will do anything to keep humanity in the dark so that he can continue to oppress them. The truth is that the power in the name of Jesus brings deliverance from all oppressions of the devil and delivers dominion to humanity. We can use the name through the agency of prayer when going through adversity and dealing with limits set over our lives in whatever form they come.

Whatever may be the case, the Lord says it is a new season for the church of God. The lord is deploying His angels to lead His people in the body of Christ into a new season. They are on white horses ready to win the battle and hand you victory through Christ. It is a period to deploy the name above all names – Jesus Christ, with this new understanding and let it work for you. Many will not understand the works of God in your life, but it is your time and season. The power in the name of Jesus can change any situation you may find yourself. The fact that there are things not going on well does not mean that things will remain as it is all the time. The enemy had succeeded in deceiving many that their suffering today is due to the sins they had committed before they became born again or even a consequence of sins of other family members. The truth is that there are generational curses, but once there is an understanding that there is a change in covenant with Christ being the guarantee of this new covenant, we can take back the power to destroy from our enemy. We appropriate the authority that is in the name of Jesus, and we can break all curses.

Even though there is consequence to our choices and decision we make, once we step out of them and come into the camp of God, He turns all of them around as we deploy the power in His name. It has to be made clear, however, that being in Christ alone and accepting Christ does not end the hostilities from Satan our arch-enemy. We would have to wrestle control from his hands. It is just like being indebted to a company, then a stranger walk into a bank and pays the debt, you no longer owe. If for any reason the company called to say you still owe them you need to supply the details of the receipt as proof of payment, and that should be it. Should the company representative proof stubborn, you still stand your ground with the particulars of the receipt of payment until they accept that you no longer owe them. So it is with our deliverance from the hands of Satan, Jesus has paid the debt and therefore anything we carried as a consequence of our being in bondage no longer has to be in our lives.

We have to stand up to the enemy with the details of our receipt which is Jesus Christ and His work to claim our liberty. The Apostles Peter and John were able to pray for the disabled beggar in the name of Jesus Christ of Nazareth to receive healing. The act was like showing the proof of payment to Satan that Jesus had paid in full for the healing and deliverance. As a result, Satan recognised it and gave way for the restoration of strength to the disabled beggar's legs to enable him to walk again.

There is no permanency to any condition as far as God is concerned if the believers correctly deploy the tools available to them. For instance, the doctor's report maybe saying it is impossible to have children, but the God of heaven through Christ can change that. I am not a medical practitioner, but I stand to reason that if paralysis can be healed in the name of Jesus Christ as in the case of the disabled beggar, without the application of medicine, then any medical condition by faith in Christ can be healed. That is not to suggest medicine is not godly because God supplies the wisdom with which scientists, pharmacologists, pharmacists and doctors and other medical practitioners do their respective work, researching, formulating and administering those drugs.

Hannah, the wife of Elkanah, was barren and was mocked by Peninnah, her rival. It happened that as Hannah went up to worship in Shiloh, she cried before the Lord and made a vow to the Lord God almighty that if he gave her a son, she would give him back to God. God granted her wish and turned Hannah's weeping into joy. He is still in the business of turning our weeping into joy. God has not changed. What he did for Hannah and Joseph, he can do for you, for as Luke 1:37, says '. . . Nothing is impossible for God.' He can heal our bodies, our minds and even change the events of our life, for nothing is impossible for Him.

There are so many places in the Bible where God changed the present of people to give a new meaning to their past. Consider all those whom he raised from the dead, the most famous and well-known being Jesus Christ himself, in the glorious resurrection. It is possible to say that in life, pain and problems come to everyone at one stage. As believers, we are encouraged knowing that God is our helper and that he will see us through life's challenges. God has promised that He will never leave us nor forsake us and that he will fight our battles. God will turn it around for your good in Christ Jesus every demonic attack you receive. God turns tests into testimony, and adversity into victorious adventure, as well as mess into a message.

God also turns people's failures into triumphs and their disappointments into divine appointments. Perhaps you have done something wrong and made some bad choices regarding your life, or maybe you have done wrong, and now you are suffering the consequences of those mistakes. Let me assure you that regardless of any mistake you have made in the past or the challenge that confronts you, if you will turn to Christ, he is prepared to take your mistakes, your awful circumstance, and convert it into a miracle.

The disabled man at the beautiful gate was an outcast; he could not mingle with people because of his disability. But through the name of God, his limitation was turned around when Peter and John met him. The power in the name of Jesus has not changed, it still works in the lives of those who connect to Christ by faith. There is enough power in the name of Jesus to break every limitation. Regardless of the circumstance, you are in, with God on your side, and all the provision available in Christ Jesus. When a man lifts you up, it's definitely at the height of his hands, but when God lifts you up, it is limitless.

Seek Christ, deploy His name to your advantage in any given circumstance and it will work for you because no situation ever remained the same when it came into contact with that name ¬Jesus Christ. It is a name, God the Father has granted the authority to wield power in all realms of life – the heavens, the universe including the earth and the realm of Satan and His cohorts. It is a name that is recognised, respected and kowtowed. He has authority over all things. Whatever the circumstances of your birth, your upbringing, your educational attainment, your health status, your credit status, these cannot dictate the course of your life when you have surrendered to the King of Kings, Jesus Christ, and He rules over your life. You will certainly emerge a winner.

Let us now look at some specific benefits that the name of Jesus brings to us.

The Power In The Name Of Jesus – The Pragmatics His Name Gives Us Our Identity

As a Christian, you are identified with God because you believe in the name of Jesus and are expected to live like Him. Jesus gives us a new identity because we have lost our own spiritual identity and standing before God through sin. When we accept Jesus Christ as Lord and saviour we are hidden in Him because we put on Christ (Galatians 3:27). We no longer live by our desire and personal philosophies, but we surrender all to Him and take on His. The implication is that He takes over the responsibility to care for us through the covenant we have with Him. Therefore, when we mention that name, He shows up with all His power and grace. Also when we are in Him, because it is no longer us who live but Christ that lives in us by faith, we take on a new identity. The disabled beggar was healed and, all the people who saw him marvelled because his status has changed. He who was once   a disabled beggar was leaping, jumping and praising God in the temple with them possibly never to go back to that sort of demeaning life anymore.

Jesus' Name Is Above Every Other Name.

The name of Jesus is above the name of any sickness or disease or situation. Peter did mention it, and through it, the man was healed (Philippians 2:9-11). If we go back to the story of the disabled beggar which is the crust of this material, Apostles Peter and John met the disabled beggar. The healing took place in the covered walkway called Solomon's Portico that is just inside the eastern section of the outer court of the Temple area. As a crowd grew around them and the former disabled beggar, Peter took the opportunity to present the gospel to the astonished throng. In so doing, he first denied that the apostles had any power to accomplish the healing that they had just witnessed. Quite the contrary, it was a testimony to the presence and power of the 'God of Abraham, Isaac, and Jacob, the God of our forefathers' who by this act had 'glorified his servant Jesus' – the very one whom the Jews had rejected. It was not a strange statement to make because, it is   a fact, of course, that the Jews commonly used this formula in their times of daily prayers. Therefore, the patriarchal formula held importance in Peter's remarks by demonstrating that Jesus was the ultimate fulfilment of Moses' teaching and thus was of supreme significance for the Jewish people— the very ones who had rejected him. Contrary to Peter pointing to Christ of the miraculous healing of the disabled beggar, I see a looming danger in certain circles of African Christianity as a whole particularly of the Pentecostal Charismatic denominations where members make statements such as 'the God of their leader' often inserting the names of their leaders. To try to address this danger calls for a very deep theological exegesis and exposition. It would be uncontainable within the space and time of this material, as it is intended for easy reading even for those without any serious theological training and skills in handling the scriptures.

The practice of referring to their God as the God of their leaders in the same vein as 'the God of Abraham' is dangerous and it is a misplaced self-glorifying act, elevating such church leaders to the level of the Patriarchs. As things go within the sphere of humankind's relationship with God the Father, every Christian can only approach Him through Christ. But for Christ, no one would be able to stand in the Father's presence whatsoever. No matter how powerful people become with a great following they do not in any way get elevated to a level of a covenant with God the Father directly, but through the covenant, we have received by the sinless birth, suffering, death, and resurrection of Christ. That is why Jesus still stands at the right hand of God the Father making intercession for us. It is for this reason; we pray in Jesus' name to the Father because Jesus Christ is the only person that qualifies to represent us in His presence. In some way, I can understand that due to the unusual things carried out through these Christian leaders by God through Christ sometimes their followers believe it is because they have some special standing with God by themselves and therefore resort to such accolades. Also because in the Old Testament such statements were made of Abraham, Isaac, and Jacob such as the God of Abraham, Christians have thought it is a statement they can make to underline their leaders' intimacy with God. The reason why Abraham, Isaac, Jacob could be referred to as such was that of the special covenant status they had with God as the patriarchs of people through whom God would eventually reveal the messiah to the world. That's why there is nowhere in the bible with statements like the God of Isaiah or Zechariah or even the God of Matthew or the God of Peter. It was all about Christ because it was the only name that was recognised and found worthy to represent His people in His presence.

Only Through His Name Can You Get Anything From God

> *"And in that day you will ask Me nothing. Most assuredly, I say to you, whatever you ask the Father in My name He will give you. 24 Until now you have asked nothing in My name. Ask, and you will receive, that your joy may be full."* *(John 16:23-24)*

The above-quoted scripture is a direct instruction from Jesus as to how those that follow him would receive anything they desire from God. They would have to ask in His name. The reason is that he has earned the authority and power in His name by His suffering and death. And Jesus knew this so well as we read in Revelations 5:1-5, as no one was worthy to break the seals of the scroll in the hand of the one that sat upon the throne but Jesus was. With boldness Jesus proclaimed, he was the way, the truth and the life and no one approached the Father but through Him. That is the audacity of a name. He is now the gateway to God and the blessing: you can only go in and get your blessings, including healing, peace, prosperity, favour, success through Him and no one else. When you even closely examine the pronouncement of blessing on Abraham from God, the grace is accentuated and accessed through Him. You can access the promised blessing of Abraham even when you are from Abraham's biological lineage by connecting to Christ. In Christ, you become grafted into the family as an heir (Galatians 3:29).

When the lame man asked Peter for alms, he responded by saying 'in the name of Jesus Christ of Nazareth rise and walk.' In effect what had happened was that the name Jesus seized the paralysis and utterly consumed it or better still swallowed it up. All that was left, was the power in the name and that meant restoration and making everything new. Jesus rose from the dead with a new life, he was easily recognisable, and when he was recognised, he insisted no one touched Him until He has presented Himself to His Father in heaven (John 20:17). And so anytime the name is super imposed on anything it must become new. Even at conversion when any individual truly accepts Jesus into their lives all things become new, old passes away (2 Corinthians 5:17). And it is all because of the new life with which he rose from the dead.

His Name Is At Work At All Times

"I am He who lives, and was dead, and behold; I am alive always. Amen. And I have the keys of Hades and Death" (Revelations 1:18)

"teaching them to observe all things that I have commanded you; and lo, I am with you always, even to the end of the age. Amen" (Matthew 28:20)

Because people's name still lives after them, mentioning some names, emotes anger, or sadness   or joy and gratitude. When one hears the name of Mother Teresa and the name Adolf Hitler, it stirs memory with emotions. Mother Teresa was a Catholic Nun of Albanian descent who worked in the slums   of Calcutta, India. She founded the Missionaries of Charity which had over 4500 sisters and operative in

133 countries around the world. Her work involved managing homes for people dying of HIV AIDS, Leprosy and Tuberculosis. On the other hand, Adolf Hitler was a German politician and leader of the Nazi Party. He was also Chancellor from 1933 to 1945 and initiated the Second World War in Europe with the invasion of Poland in September 1939. He was a central figure in the Holocaust ordering the massacre of over 6 million Jews, 1.5 million being children, a genocide of seismic proportions never seen in the history of human kind. There could be some emotions of fondness attached to the name Mother Teresa and anger attached to Adolf Hitler by the mere mention of their names. Jesus' name does not only stirs, joy, peace, love and some fondness but there is power in that name. When mentioned there is a similar reaction and response because it is a recognisable name in all realms of life, both terrestrial and celestial.

Jesus Christ still lives, His name and the power it exerts is still present. His life still speaks for a countless number of people around the world with testimonies. Jesus has authority from the Father to rule over all things. Because Jesus lives forever and He is with us always, the power in His name is ever present to help in time of our need. Look for Him, or call Him anytime, anywhere and the authority in the name will work. Peter and John did not send the man to a special place for him to be healed or waited for a particular time of deliverance before exercising the authority that name has over the condition of the disabled beggar. The result was the miracle the disabled beggar experienced, beyond his wildest dream and expectations.

The Enemy Knows And Understands The Power Of Name Jesus

I have made mention of the fact that, the name of Jesus is recognisable in both realms of life - the physical and spiritual. We would explore some of the practical examples of scripture, where the indication is given of the sort of response and reaction to the presence and mention of the name of Jesus. We would examine the scriptures below:

> *"And suddenly they cried out, saying, "What have we to do with You, Jesus, You Son of God? Have You come here to torment us before the time?" (Matthew 8:29).*

"And this she did for many days. But Paul, greatly annoyed, turned and said to the spirit, "I command you in the name of Jesus Christ to come out of her." And he got out that very hour." (Acts 16:18)

From the above scriptures, it is the demons inhabiting the mentally deranged man living in the tombs of a cemetery who announced the presence of Jesus Christ on the shores of that city of the Gadarenes. They recognised Jesus as having the authority and power to break their hold on the man and their work in that particular geographical location. They protested out of discomfort of the presence of Jesus in that area although He has not uttered a word at the time, because they recognised Him as someone with the authority and power over them.

If we look once again at the second scripture quotation above, we again realise the demon that worked through the young woman that followed Paul and the other disciple had recognised Christ in them and was uncomfortable, knowing that the Christ in whose name Paul preached had authority and power over it. The demon through the young woman devised a strategy to distract the servants of God and people from presenting Jesus. There is no question whatsoever that demons trembled at the presence of Jesus and the name of Jesus. The evil power of every adversity and limits on your life would succumb to the name of Jesus when appropriated. Command healing or deliverance over your life or loved one in the name of Jesus and there would be a reaction.

You must be willing to demonstrate your confidence in God's ability in every circumstance you find yourself. You need to face your problems and say: "God is able." Stop presenting God as a weak, impotent and unresponsive force to the challenges of your life. He is a God of power – He impacts every situation and circumstance, changes lives, destinies, and delivers, He heals and saves. He can deliver you from all the forces that are up against you (Psalms 34:17). If He parted the red sea, fell the wall of Jericho, he has never changed, He can do it again and again through Jesus Christ.

You must also be confident in your ability. Not only is God powerful, but you are also, in Christ. You have the power through Christ to break through limiting forces of life (Luke 10:19). Stop looking helpless and powerless. You are a mighty man of valour just like Gideon and Jephthah. Joseph overcame all the odds against him and rose to be a prime minister because of God's presence in his life. You are a Woman of great conquest just like Deborah and Jael; your enemies will fall at your feet through exercising the authority and power through Jesus Christ.

Whatever you may be going through; whatever problems you are encountering, whatever threatens to overwhelm you – God can bring you through it. Besides, you also have been empowered through Christ to overcome life's challenges. The adversity or challenges you face is a force strong enough to abort the plan and purpose of God for you and your family. Through Christ, you can, and you will rise above the storms and be who God says you are. Give up your helplessness and tap into the unlimited potential you carry on the inside for therein lies the key to your breakthrough.

The Name Of Jesus Is A Strong Refuge.

"The name of the Lord is a strong tower; Therighteous run to it and are safe." (Proverbs 18:10)

In this verse, the name of YHVH is likened to Migdal Oz – the 'strong tower' that was used as the chief fortification for a city in the ancient times. For the tzaddik – the righteous man who calls upon the name of the Lord – God is an all-powerful defence in times of peril. The metaphor suggests the righteous man running into an immensely fortified tower, being elevated above the surrounding danger. The Lord is a tower for those who put their trust in Him.

The essence for us in the post-New Testament era is that The Hebrew name Yehoshua derives from a combination of YHVH and Yasha, and means 'YHVH saves.' Later Yehoshua was shortened to Yeshua (Nehemiah 8:17), which is the Hebrew name for Jesus. As a type of Joshua, Jesus exemplifies the ultimate deliverance of His people, by taking Israel into the land to inherit the promises. Indeed, calling upon the name of the Lord Jesus is to call upon the name of YHVH, since Jesus Himself is YHVH come in the flesh (Isaiah 9:6; 45:23; Philippians 2:11; Romans 10:9). There is no other name given to humankind for salvation other than the name Jesus (Acts 4:12; Isaiah 43:11).

The power in the name provides protection, covering for them that believe in it. When you call His name in the time of danger, Jesus' over-riding presence envelopes you and quickly shields you from any imminent evil immediately.

His Name Commands Instant Delivery

"...In the name of Jesus Christ of Nazareth, rise and walk." 7 And he took him by the right hand and lifted him up, and immediately his feet and ankle bones received strength." (Acts 3:6-7)

Just when the Apostles prayed and commanded in Jesus name for the disabled beggar to rise and walk, they took him by their hand to help him to obey the command because they knew very well, that was not his expectation and also to avoid him sitting there doubting their charge against his infirmity.

When you call His name for help, He dispatches the answer immediately. Most of the time you see an instant manifestation, but some other times you see the result after a while as you walk in obedience to God's word. Whatever the experience may be, the bottom line is that so long as there is a reaction in both realms of life, there is bound to be a result. The focus here is not to give reasons why some results are instant or others gradual. However, the point I am making clear here is that the name works when invoked and called to action in a time of need. There is no laid down formulae for calling on the name of the Lord, but if you call Jesus' name in unbelief, you may not obtain the desired results. Therefore, anytime you are mentioning Jesus' name do it in faith and with the understanding of the power that lies in His name. Peter did it with faith that is why the disabled's feet gained strength.

You Must Have A Relationship With Jesus

It is very dangerous to use the name of Jesus if you have not identified with Him or accepted Him as Lord and saviour. You have to give your life to Jesus first and have a relationship with him before you can exercise authority with the power in the name. Let see an example of the sons of a Chief Priest, called Sceva (see below). They attempted to use the name of Christ 'the one Paul preaches' in a deliverance session with a demon-possessed person, and the results were catastrophic. They were over-powered by the demon on the basis that they recognised the spiritual authority of Paul to use the name of Jesus against them but by whose authority do they exercise the use of that name.

> "And the evil spirit answered and said, "Jesus I know, and Paul I know; but who are you?" Then the man in whom the evil spirit leaped on them, overpowered[b] them, and prevailed against them,[c] so that they fled out of that house naked and wounded. This became known both to all Jews and Greeks dwelling in Ephesus, and fear fell on them all, and the name of the Lord Jesus was magnified." (Acts 19:13-17)

As people in the body of Christ, if we obey his word, we will be able to exercise power in His name. However, some people pray for God's blessings, but the moment they start experiencing them, they begin to abandon the house of God and begin to focus on acquiring material things. In my assessment, I think the church has become overly materialistic and could account for the pursuit of materialism other than Christ. There is a breakdown of real commitment to God through Christ, and it is indicative of how people make vows to God when they are in trouble, but when they are out of it, they forget about their promises with God. Sometimes they find excuses; I have to take care of my children, my salary is not enough to give ten percent, or I do not close early from work to attend prayer meetings. Some people when they are in difficulties or challenges, are punctual in the house of God, but when things start to get better, they begin to give excuses. As a matter, of course, one could find very legitimate palpable excuses why they cannot show and exhibit a bit more commitment to the Kingdom of God and of His Christ.

God wants us to walk in obedience to His word and our vow. It is our obedience that strengthens our relationship with Him and builds a stronger bond of acquaintance. When we have a more robust relationship with an acquaintance then, anytime we call upon Him, He shows up. When God has said something and delivered on the promise, it is not the time to be disobedient and complacent, but time to continue with your commitment or even perfect it to receive more from Him, unfortunately, it is not the case sometimes. It is the time to rise and walk your talk with Him and talk your walk with Him.

CHAPTER SIX

RISE UP AND WALK

The disabled beggar was confronted by a situation far more than he bargained. He only asked for alms and yet was about to receive something much more than he had requested which was not only going to take care of His present need but deal with the root of the circumstances which was his paralysis. It was the intention of the Apostles to help the disabled man deal with his situation permanently by tackling the limitation and not just the challenges the limitation posed to him on a daily basis.

In the end, after they prayed for him, he still sat there probably because the whole experience was novel to him and a bit too much for him and didn't know what next he needed to do. Peter and John knew the release of power in the name of Christ to him, and there was no reason he should be sitting and so aided him to rise to his feet. And just when he cooperated and stood up he realised he had strength in his legs and was able to stand. To be sure and out of joy, he started walking, jumping, and leaping from one place to the other praising God. We would continue analysing the story from three different perspectives as done through the book. We would examine it from the disabled beggar's perspective, from the Apostles perspective and the perspective of the reader of the story. The focus of this chapter at this point is the circumstances that surround His rising, the actual act of rising and walking.

One of the problems with most people is that they sit complain about the barriers that surround them but do not make an attempt to overcome them even when they have prayed. As though after they have prayed things would automatically fall in place without their cooperation to make what they seek come to them. Let us clarify this point because some have felt that once they get involved in the process the outcome would not be of God anymore. For instance, when you pray to God in an exam for success, it does not mean you don't have to study. Yours is to study and also back it all up with prayer and leave the rest to God to deliver the success. God's part is all the things He may do in the background, behind the scenes which you may not be able to imagine, to deliver the success to you. I have undertaken different levels of tertiary level education and also taught courses at tertiary level as a lecturer. I know that no two essays are marked the same by two different lecturers, the marks awarded by these two different markers must be within a certain acceptable range. One marker could assign an A and the other a B which makes a lot of difference in academia in the student's Cumulative Grade Point Average(CGPA). So the point here is that God's involvement may not even be so clear cut and could use different circumstances to deliver the answer to your prayer for success in an examination. An understanding of the nature of awarding marks to an essay, may equally apply in different areas of life. When you commit something into the hands of the Lord, your responsibility is to take care of all that is humanly possible, your responsibility is not automatically absorbed by the prayer. That would be gross irresponsibility. Often good-hearted but weak minded individuals expect something to occur beyond their contribution to make it all happen for them because God is involved. Truly speaking, it does not work that way.

To a vast extent, this is how it works, but that is not to say that God does deliver answers to prayer sometimes without the involvement of people, or even sometimes circumvent the effort of the one that prayed and provide answers without any effort or involvement of the one that prayed. There are also a lot of examples and testimonies to that effect. However, that is not for anyone who prays to shirk their responsibilities in doing all that is humanly possible on their part in any endeavour they undertake. Like the disabled beggar, you would need to rise from your sitting. If you want anything in life, you have to rise to get it. There are some of us that have sat for too long and become used to sitting that even when there are opportunities all around us, we do not see because it is not falling on our lap. It has to take an effort from us.

Sometimes in education, you come across courses, topics, and subjects that are very much unfamiliar which you wish you never registered to attend. There are even some of them you could envisage would be difficult, but it is an unavoidable and necessary part of the programme of study. You have no choice but to brace yourself to attend and study it. You couldn't ask someone else to take it up for you because it simply does not work like that. No, you have to tuck into the course or topic or subject yourself. Even though it may be difficult to study and may not come naturally to you, you engage the discipline mode and get on with it. With some practice, you can overcome the barriers and fulfil its requirement for a pass. There are instances you come across students who by the time they are half way through the course have themselves become teachers and helpers to some of their colleagues on the course.

We have just discussed an instance where people shirk their responsibilities to rise and get on with life, but we would also not lose sight of the fact that there are those who don't even know what to do. Having said that, the result of knowing what to do and not doing it and not knowing what to do are the same; it is a life of zero productivity and fruitfulness. It yields the same results of being where you are of where you used to be. The same place!

As earlier indicated, it is my view that the disabled beggar was a little overwhelmed by the whole situation and maybe blown away, that he didn't even know what to do after he had received prayer. Someone would, however, argue that should rather have been the impetus to jump at the chance of being healed permanently and not coming to sit at the beautiful gate to depend on the benevolence of those going to the temple daily. There is a danger that sometimes people go through certain difficulties for a long time, and after they have tried so many times to get out to no avail, they don't expect a change anymore and just live with the situation. That could also be an explanation to acquiesce.

Deep within the disabled beggar, he had circumstantially become content with his condition, but when Peter made him aware that he needs to rise, he did and   got results. The lame man had carried a limitation throughout his life with no hope; he had accepted it as his way of life. You could have a limitation in your life that you will desire no change anymore because you have become so used to that kind of life. God has given us the opportunity to the life that we live and the choices we make. We need to be responsible for the life that we make and stop complaining. Many have found stories to exonerate themselves of why they are in such a bad situation. It is time for you to recognise that it may be a limitation upon your life but you have to make a choice to stay with the limitation or break away from it.

The disabled beggar was not sure of the results of the prayer of the apostles. It is not even clear he even believed in what the power of God could do at all. Maybe he was just playing along so that in the end he could have a few coins. It is also possible he was caught unawares by the whole situation and didn't have much of choice but just followed instructions. Whatever the case may be, as soon as you are willing to do whatever it takes to become successful at any endeavour or break bounds to explore yonder a new horizon, and bring yourself to do whatever it takes, success would come knocking at the door. As soon as you stop erecting barriers to your ideal life, and go into action with the attitude that you are willing to do whatever it takes, you will succeed. There was a young woman who shared her story on ABC's(US

Television Network) 20/20 program which was very inspiring. The woman had lost both of her legs above the knee but was determined to walk on two prostheses even when the doctors said it would be impossible. Through further surgery, stretching her remaining muscle over theend of the bone on her legs and special prosthesis, she overcame her limitation and can walk. She had a spirit that wouldn't die, a determination and tenacity to walk again, and it happened. What does that say to you? You need to know how to overcome your limitations and be successful in every area of your life.

Rising Right Where You Are

An underlining theme subtly presented in this material as a way to deal with your adversity and break limits has been tackling them from the root. That is to say, without being repetitive, that to identify the limitations that produce the challenges that need attention all the time. The disabled beggar's focus was on dealing with his adversity by begging while the real solution he needed was healing from his paralysis that has made him unable to work by himself to make a decent living. God is most of the time looking at how He will break the limitation in our lives so as to be able to deal with our challenges or problems that come to us. You may be complaining about how to get a better job, but your limitation may be how to acquire new skills to improve on your current job so that you can earn more without even changing jobs. Or better still get a skill set required by the current job market but within your area of interest, ability and expertise. Your competence and area of interest would help you find a new job.

Also, another thing that also makes people unable to see the manifestation of God's blessings in their lives is that they keep on sitting down even when the limitations break because of the condition they are in, and the length of time they have suffered the condition. They expect some special treatment rising out of sympathy from God and the people around them to do what they needed anyhow without any involvement at all from them. The lame man least expected Peter to ask him to rise and walk because he had lived in that state for a long time. What he did not understand was that it was in that same state that he needed to rise irrespective of the history and story behind his disability and his perceived inability to walk. That is why some people say they have prayed and God has not yet answered their prayers. God might have removed the limitation that brings the challenge in their lives, but they have not realised it because they have not made an effort to rise. To test the limitation is broken was to rise to see if his legs were able to carry the rest of his body.

Until you make that effort to rise you would not be able to have the experience, and would still be seated when you are meant to be walking, and leaping. It is always necessary to first rise and not remain seated for whatever might have placed you in that seating position. There are times that some of the limitations that people face is spiritual. And so it makes it difficult to realise it is gone, but the only way to determine they are broken or not is to do what you once did and failed, see what the results could be this time around. It is your responsibility to arise and walk because God has already broken the chains and declared you free. When Peter and John lifted up the lame man, he immediately felt the strength in his feet and ankle. Until they fed the mind with new information and instruction, he remained in his position till he was helped to walk. His mind has not changed to accept that change is possible in the power of almighty in his life. To move from your current position may be just changing your mind; how you arrive at a particular decision and think about things.

Renewing The Mind

The human mind is like a ceiling of a building. How high you can think and reason will determine how high you will go in life. No one can rise above their mental capabilities. How free your mind can express itself in thinking and reasoning determines how open you live your life. Some people think that they are still in bondage whereas they have been freed. The disabled beggar had been prayed for and healed, and instead of rising and taking charge of his new found freedom he still sat there. There are people like that in life who have been blessed one way or the other for a better, higher and greater life of purpose but they remain seated. It is up to them to rise and change the way they think and they would realise they see differently. Some would even suddenly realise their problems were long gone. Some people hold a particular perception about various aspects of life that makes it difficult for them to become successful at one thing or the other. That is not in any way to suggest that, there is a particular perception one needs to hold to be successful, as success itself is relative. What is true however is, understanding the whole concept of perception and its ramifications to enable you to switch and balance when necessary for the desired outcome in any endeavour of life is good.

Perception is the way we look at things from our point of view. It is the mental lens through which we look at everything in our surroundings and interact with them in a particular way unique to us. Your perception could either imprison your future and provide the impetus for a quantum leap in accomplishment. In simple terms, if you were to pour a bottle fluid of a litre volume into a two-litre bottle, there is a possibility of obtaining two different approaches to describing the content of its container. You will have a description of it being half empty and another description as half full. The answers are based on perception. The first description of my analysis is from a scarcity mind-set while the second is from an abundance perspective. None of the two stories can be said to be wrong within the context of the sample. However, it says so much about how these two persons with these descriptions of the sample would perceive opportunities. When an individual is fixated on a problem even when within the problem is a solution, they miss it. The disabled beggar was fixated on his disability and not the possibility of a solution, and so after being prayed for when it was expected of him to rise and walk he still sat, he had to be extended a helping hand. He should see an opportunity to take his life back to recover the years lost to the disability.

Rene Descartes, a 16th-century French Philosopher in explaining the role of perception, uses an illustration of an analogue black and white photo camera. He states that the colour we see of an object, may not necessarily be a property of the object. Rather, a combination of factors makes us see the object in that colour. Meaning, pictures taken with an analogue black and white photo camera would give you pictures in black and white, although the object may be in colour. So the reason for the change in the colours of the object taken with the camera is simply the receptors of the camera which is in black and white. It is the lenses with which we look at things that determine how we see them. The way our minds are programmed determines whether we see opportunity when we are presented with one as opportunity or not. The chance to rise may not come to you the way you want to see it unless you probably change the receptors with which you capture your mental images. Your ability to rise lies in how you see.

Another thing that perception affect is our choice of what we consider important. Sometimes changing your perception helps you to improve your value systems to a productive one. Value systems are your standards and discipline set, based on the common sense and wisdom of knowing what the proper moral rules and discipline are, and the amount of willingness to see yourself and others abide by them. In short, values are informed by the things you consider important in your life. The difficulty with some people is that they want God to bless them when as a matter of fact, they are supposed to renew their mind. The renewing of the mind would help them to see differently and discover they are already blessed, and required to rise. They would have to change their perception when necessary in line with how God sees the situation. Some of the things that you place value on in your life and how you negotiate with those must change to conform with the things God places value on if you want God to respond in a way you so desire. There must be an alignment of values to expect God to move in a particular way in your life. Some people spend countless hours on their pastime while less on things that will build them for the life they desire. What do you value most? Your past time or the building blocks required to erect a magnificent building of life. And yet they expect to be great achievers and high fliers in their careers and jobs. They aspire to be great people in future, but they do not want to pay the price of great men by prioritising what is more valuable to them. They wish to be on top, but they do not want to do what those people did before they got to the high place. The secret of most managers and chief executives of excelling companies; pastors of effective churches; professors with astute research credentials are not only there because of their certificates of education but their value systems aided by developing the right perception.

Many people are successful not only because they have gone through years of advanced education but because they have developed the right kind of perception of the things they excel in. You may get opportunities to destroy limitations in your life, whether using prayer, debt cancellation, education, financial capital but most of the time, you need to rise and walk when all is set and done. Your refusal to arise may keep you in that same place. When we expect something special to happen in our lives, we need to do something special. We cannot do the same things or the things we used to do and expect something different. You cannot, therefore, maintain the same mind-set as the framework of analysis in every situation and plan to arrive at different outcomes. What goes in, is what comes out in the end. In biblical language, you reap what you sow (Galatians 6:7).

From the perspective of God, He lives in a spirit realm and so what He does is in the spirit. We have to be sensitive enough to download spiritual information and take the necessary physical steps needed. We sometimes blame God for our woes. Meanwhile, He has done it in the spirit, it up to us to rise and walk. Do not wait for everything around you to be assured before you move even though you may not feel anything but with faith; you can rise and walk. You may be having a dream, but your dream will never be a reality if you do not act on it. Apostles Peter and John helped the man because they realise that he did not have the understanding of what was going on. Do not wait for a prophecy, for example, to be given about your dream before you act although that could help, move now. Remember it is God who works in you both to will and act according to His purpose for your life. The great heights which men reached and kept were not achieved by sudden flight but they while their companions slept, they were toiling upwards in the night. They rose up to do what most of their companions were not ready to do then. Once God has placed a desire in you, you have the responsibility to make a move. Do not wait for all the conditions to be right before you move. What you need to know is for you to decide to act - rise and walk as there may never be a perfect time for an action. If life will be good for you, it depends on you. Not the current difficult economic situation can stop you from excelling and succeeding. No matter the crisis and the hardships, others are making it and so can you. If those making headway in the same conditions have complained, they would not have been where they are now. You need to be able to take responsibility for your life. You cannot always blame others for your life. God has done his part, you need to do yours, and you will begin to see the manifestation of God's blessing in your life.

The 'Curse' Of The Right Time

One of the common statements you often hear from a believer is 'God's time is the best.' The problem is not that the declaration is false in itself, but the problem is that many hide behind that and do nothing. The right time is to rise when all is set and done. There is a story found in 2 Kings 7:1-10, in the scripture, the four lepers whether they were aware of the prophecy of Elisha or not found themselves in the centre of the fulfilment of prophecy because they perceived rightly and were willing to rise irrespective of their disability. It was their decision to rise to go to the Syrian army's camp in search for food even at the peril of their lives that became the source of the breakthrough for the whole nation. It was not exactly clear how the fulfilment of the prophecy was going to be, although it was going to happen imminently. That is to say, the provision for the overflow was available, but somehow someone had to rise and make a move to trigger the release of the overflow. Even though it looked like God has won the battle over famine for them, they had to rise and go for the victory. No one ever told them the Syrians would flee from their camp, but they made a bold decision to go to the camp.

They did not fight the Syrian army, but the army fled as a result of a divine act where God amplifies the sound of the footsteps of the lepers. In the end, only four lepers defeated the entire Syrian army. They had been leprous men, dying from starvation, shut out from the city, waiting to die until they found themselves at the centre of a dramatic turn-around in the fortunes of the nation. They reasoned and thought about their situation. They said, "Why sit we here until we die?" They rose up and went - and got what they needed. God providentially prepared before them all that their hearts desired. Sometimes fear keeps us in our comfort zone of inactivity and deprivation. We do not want to move because we are afraid of failing, and failure to move means we cannot experience what is on the other side. The irony of our fear is that most of the time, they do not exist. We need to put fear aside to rise and move forward. If the lepers had looked at their condition, they would have sat and died. They gathered courage and moved on.

The issue of fear reminds me of a friend I met while in school. We had all arrived in the country as international students and needed a laptop to assist us in our assignments, and research work. I went to PC World to purchase one on credit, and I briefed him of how he can also acquire one. He wondered how possible as a migrant student I was able to approach such a reputable company to purchase an item on credit. The problem I had with him was that he was having all the necessary documents to stay in the United Kingdom but his uncle who has been an illegal immigrant for years in the country brainwashed him into believing that when he goes near such places, he is likely to be arrested and deported. Even though he was legally permitted to stay in the UK, this information from His uncle made him live like an illegal immigrant forfeiting all the benefits he could have enjoyed but for fear.

Sometimes we do not look for the opportunities ourselves, but we rely on what others say. We have accepted the old information without adjusting to the new ways of doing things. If the lepers at the gate of Samaria had waited for a cue from someone before moving, they would have remained at the gate and died there. The four lepers considered they had nothing to lose, and they made it.

In situations where we need the help of God, and we call on Him we need to believe, He has done it and therefore need to rise up. Whatever dream you have, rise up and pursue it and it will surely come to fruition. Never wait to realise that it is too late to rise up and walk.

CHAPTER SEVEN

GIVING THANKS, PRAISING GOD

As the disabled man was lifted up by the Apostles, He stood up on his feet, started walking and then leaping about and praising God. Praise is about telling what the Lord has done with a sense of gratitude expressed in actions and with words. It carries within it an expression of approval or admiration of the blessings received, works and benefits. To this end, we now understand why the disabled beggar, stood and started walking and then leaping around praising God. For many believers of our time, praising God has been limited to verbalising gratitude and also screaming, shouting, raising hands among others, and if you consider the essence of genuine praise, it is to put on show what the Lord has done for you.

Doing what you could not do before you received from God. That alone generated a sense of awe among those that knew about the condition before the time of the receipt of the blessing. It is not to downgrade the place and essence of verbalising praise and its associated actions because they are all biblical, but the emphasis is to combine them all effectively as a witness to the graciousness of God. The will of God in Christ Jesus is to give thanks to God in everything. Every believer should know why we should give thanks and be grateful all the time. Gratitude is a feeling of thankfulness and appreciation of everything the Almighty God is doing in our daily lives. The single greatest act of worship you can render to God is to thank Him. It's the epitome of worship because, through gratitude, we affirm God as the ultimate source of both our trials and blessings. With a thankful heart, you can say in the midst of anything, "God be praised." That kind of attitude looks beyond the circumstance to the plan of God. It sees beyond the pain to the sovereignty of God. As Paul tell the church in Thessalonica;

"in everything give thanks; for this is the will of God in Christ Jesus for you." (1 Thessalonians 5:18)

We thank God for those natural things (body, earthy) that He has done or will do. We praise God because our soul (intellect, emotions, etc...) recognises His sovereignty and other divine attributes. We worship Him with our spirit, for God is a Spirit and they that worship Him must worship Him in spirit and truth. The lame man showed a trilogy composition of these three acts of appreciation and adoration (thanksgiving, praise, and worship). It is a requirement of God to always to give thanks to God when He does something for us. We should not wait to give Him thanks at the end of the year. You should learn to celebrate God for the good things He does in your life to welcome more in your life. We thank, praise and worship because God cannot praise or worship Himself so He requires us to reciprocate the good things He does for us with thanksgiving. A challenge to our materialistic world is that, because we are always looking out for more in life we are never content or satisfied enough to be thankful. We tend to quickly switch to looking up to God for the next big thing and fail to give a commensurate thanksgiving and praise He deserves adequately.

I once made an observation in an academic institution I studied. There was this particular member of the faculty who was quite close to the Vice Chancellor; I later understood why he became close and was able to maintain his closeness to Vice Chancellor. This particular faculty member was often made an MC at official events, and gush out about the virtues and able leadership of the vice chancellor, sometimes even considered by other members of the faculty to be a bit over the top. I observed this over for the years I was in that institution, and my conclusion was that this particular faculty member had the privilege of playing that role because of his approval and acknowledgment of the Vice Chancellors work with the institution. I think there are similarities with the way things work with God too, it is proven with a lot of examples from the scriptures. It is important to clarify that, humans exploit the act of praise as a political stunt in pursuance of an individuals' agenda, God wants us to honour Him as a matter of principle because He made us for that purpose but not as though He needs it to survive or be who He is. King David knew how to praise God; he found favour in the sight of God even when he sinned. More than half of the songs King David composed recorded in the Book of Psalms was praise and thanksgiving to Yahweh.

Praise, thanksgiving, and worship are not limited to only being expressed in church. It is also understandable that when people are in some form of difficulty, they tend to run to church, a designated place of prayer referred to as the House of God, and so equally when there is a blessing, it is expressed in the same location. In so doing it stirs up faith in people with similar conditions or testifies of the present working power of God for those who trust Him and rely on Him. The disabled beggar expressed his praise and thanksgiving by entering the temple to showcase what the Lord has done. For some reason, some people are ashamed to even to testify of what God has done in their lives. Those in Christ, who expect more from the Lord would have to grow beyond that and make it a habit of giving testimonies of what God has done. We should never be ashamed of the goodness of God in our lives. As already established in the chapter dealing with power in the name of Jesus, we realised we all go through Christ to Yahweh as none qualifies to stand before Him on their terms, it is He who testifies to us in the presence of God on our behalf. And it is for that reason Jesus said;

> *"Therefore whoever confesses Me before men, him I will also confess before My Father who is in heaven. But whoever denies Me before men, him I will also deny before My Father who is in heaven."*
> *(Matthew 10:32-33)*

Praising God should be our habit. We should be able to praise Him in all our endeavours continually (Psalm 34:1-3). Some people praise God at particular days and times, and there is nothing wrong with that. However, praise, thanksgiving, and worship can be a lifestyle. The more we praise, thank and worship the Lord the closer He gets to us and the more He releases His blessings into our lives. That is to say that every form of expression of praise, thanksgiving, and worship attracts the one it is directed at, as God is enthroned in his praises (Psalm 22:3). We must devote our lives to songs that eulogise God and because the songs attract the object to whom those songs are sung. If the songs eulogise God then it attracts God to the place of the praise, thanksgiving and worship.

As I have stated earlier in this chapter, there is an order that we follow to step into the blessing of His presence. It must always begin with thanksgiving; then we transition into praise, which opens the door to worship. Psalms 100:4 says;

"Enter into his gates with thanksgiving, and into his courts with praise: be thankful unto him, and bless his name."

Psalms 100:4 speaks of Thanksgiving as the invitation to get into the gates, and praise to access the courts, yet to get into His presence (Holy of Holies) where He dwells, it requires worship (they that worship Him must do so in spirit and truth). Thanksgiving has to do with what God has done (we thank God for things that He has done in the past, present, and future). Praise has to do with who God is (His majestic attributes). Worship has to do with devotion, intimacy, and relationship. Let us look at how to express our appreciation to the glory of God:

Entering His Gates With Thanksgiving And His Courts With Praise.

As seen from Psalms 100:4, we are to enter into His gates with thanksgiving and His courts with praise. At the gates, we thank God for all that He has done. Thanksgiving has to do with you and God. What He has done for you, how He has helped you and answered a personal request. Anyone can give thanks to God, for He lets it rain on the just (justified) and the unjust alike, so all have a reason to thank Him (Matthew 5:45).

Hebrews 13:15 tells us of this, it reads;

"Therefore by Him let us continually offer the sacrifice of praise to God, that is, the fruit of our lips, giving thanks to His name." You can praise God for who He is and what He has done (through His divine attributes of self-sacrificial giving) in sacrificing or giving His only begotten Son (Jesus Christ), for the remission of our sins. Praise involves a total surrender of the expression of gratitude to make it all about the object to whom it is directed. A life of praise is a surrendered life when it is all about the one to whom the praise belongs. Jesus sacrifice was an act of praise from the Son towards the Father, yet for the benefit of humanity. He had yielded His life completely to God the Father. It is in praise that we are over-awed by our human frailty to the power of

God, in that process we rededicate ourselves to God by repenting of our sins and consequently receiving forgiveness through Jesus Christ. Anyone can enter the gates, yet it is by the courts that a person is required to sacrifice, there is a giving up of one's life as you stand in awe and submission to God's works through His works. Again, praise is a sacrifice. Praise must involve emptying and making oneself of no reputation to give all that belongs to God to Him. Praise also has to do with you recognising the need to honour God, because of who He is and His divine attributes and not out of convenience. Anyone can offer praise, yet only those who are willing to sacrifice can enter praise.

Again, people offer praise when they see the acts of God that no one else can do or replicate. The spontaneous offer of praise was the case in the Book of Daniel with King Nebuchadnezzar. He did not serve God, yet when He saw the attributes of God, including His excellent power, he praised God. Daniel 2:47 tells us; "The king answered Daniel, and said, "Truly your God is the God of gods, the Lord of kings, and a revealer of secrets since you could reveal this secret." King Nebuchadnezzar began to praise God through his words, because of the revelation that God gave through the Prophet Daniel regarding the king's dream.

Stepping into the Temple For Worship

Many times as individuals, as well as in Church services we do only thanksgiving and praise. We must go all the way into worship to fully bring the presence of the Living God. Aiden Wilson Tozer, an American preacher, once said: "Without worship, we go about miserable." Throughout the Bible, I have found thanksgiving and praise in the same scripture, yet never thanks or thanksgiving and worship. You cannot get to worship without going through each step. Anyone, both Christian and non-Christian alike can thank God, or offer praise to God (give Him honour), yet only the good Christian can worship God.

Worship has to do with relationship, and there can be no connection with God outside of righteousness, in which only the Christian has because of Christ's sacrifice. Why do you think the disabled beggar went into the temple? The answer is that he wanted to worship God. He could have   run into the street or his house, but he entered the temple first. Worship is not just a physical action or acknowledgement. You cannot get to it by just raising your hands, or saying "I worship you, Lord." To get into worship you must come to the lavers (basins) at the place of praise, wherein you repent of your sins and cleansed by the precious blood of Jesus. Worship requires relationship and intimacy which happens in the presence of God. You step into God's presence through worship.

In worship, some things happen that cannot take place in the other areas. It is in worship that we receive from the Spirit of God, as well as get spiritual empowerment. When we step into worship, we are in the presence of the Lord, and it is in this holy place that we get spiritual directions, spiritual breakthrough, spiritual strategies, spiritual empowerment, etc. Worship crosses the boundaries of the mind (soul or psyche), causing us to receive from the Spirit of God.

Many think that worship is a physical posture or a physical act as I have stated above, but it is not; rather it is a spiritual attitude or act of total surrender or submission (of will). Neither does worship have to do with a person's words. Worship may cause you to say something; yet saying something does not mean that you are in worship. Worship is not just a vanishing act, but it must be a lifestyle. Worship speaks of full surrender, and not just recognising what God has done (Thanksgiving), or who He is (praise). When you live your life in total surrender to the Lord in righteousness and holiness, then your life becomes one of worship. Thus you are a worshipper. Again, worship requires the sacrifice of your entire life.

In Genesis 22:5, Abraham tells his men that he and his son will go and worship the Lord and return. This worship was sacrifice, it reads;

"And Abraham said to his young men, "Stay here with the donkey; the lad and I will go yonder and worship, and we will come back to you."

We know that Abraham's intent was to go and sacrifice Isaac on the altar, as an act of worship or total surrender to the will of God. It is the worshipper that hears the voice of the Lord. God speaks to the spirit man through worship. Many do not hear from God on a regular basis because they only have moments or seasons of worship. Those who surrender their lives to the Lord constantly hear from God more regularly, because it is in worship that God speaks to us.

You need to worship and praise God for what He has done for you from the bottom of your heart, and it will compel Him to continue to shower His blessing on you.

Jesus in Luke 17:11-17, approve the act of thanksgiving. He was pleased with the gesture of thanksgiving expressed by the healed leper. Jesus wished all ten lepers would have done the same, but they took their joy elsewhere. Jesus wants us to be like the leper who gave him all the praise and adoration before considering any other thing. He prioritised going back to the person through whom the healing came before going anywhere else including probably visiting family whom he might not have seen in a long time because lepers lived in colonies, often on the outskirts of the towns or cities. Some people always want to achieve greater things before they give thanks to God. God wants us to give him thank at all times.

> *"a woman came to Him having an alabaster flask of very costly fragrant oil, and she poured it on His head as He sat at the table. But when His disciples saw it, they were indignant, saying, "Why this waste? For this fragrant oil might have been sold for much and given to the poor." But when Jesus was aware of it, He said to them, "Why do you trouble the woman? For she has done a good work for Me." Matthew 26:7-10*

The woman in the above scripture appreciated what Christ did for her. She expressed her thanks in pouring fragrance on Jesus' feet. She put her glory and the dignity at the feet of Jesus. We should show appreciation to our God any time we receive from Him, and God will continue to shower His blessings on us. Jesus told the woman that her preachers would mention her anywhere they preach the gospel.

We need to show our thanksgiving in our offerings, commitment and obligations to the House of God you belong wherever that may be. Always remember what the Lord has done and that should keep you in a mode of thanksgiving. One of the things that remind me of thanksgiving is an escape from what could have been a fatal accident. I escaped by inches being run over by a lorry at a very high speed on my way to school many years ago. You should know that there are others who have not had or reach where you are so do not complain. Many of your peers are dead, drunks, paralysed, homeless, sectioned under the Mental Health Act, and so on. The thought of others misfortune should even urge you or give you enough reason to give God thanks and praise. You may not have been disabled like the beggar whom the Apostles John and Peter met, but there is always something you can be grateful to God for and give him praise. Whether you are strong or weak, life offers much to enjoy and many ways to serve God and be thankful to Him.

The Spiritual Weapons of Praise and Worship

Praise, thanksgiving, and worship are also weapons of spiritual warfare. Living a life of praise is not only the most enjoyable way to live, but it's also one of the most powerful ways to change your life. In spiritual warfare, our enemy is unseen, and therefore we employ weapons that may be harmless physically but very potent spiritually as spirit entities understand. It is the case because the realm of spirit is governed quite differently and may not make much sense to us in this realm. Apostle Paul said that "the weapons of our warfare are not carnal, but mighty through God to the pulling down of strong holds" (2 Corinthians 10:9). You cannot fight a spiritual enemy with natural weapons. We must use spiritual weapons of war to combat our spiritual enemy. Praise and worship are great weapons you can use to defeat the enemy in every situation. You should not only rely on fasting and prayer to get through adversity or to break any limits on your life. You should realise that genuine praise, thanksgiving, and worship carries strong power to achieve great results. There was a time that Jehoshaphat King of Judah had come under attack from Moab and Ammon, the whole of Judah came to inquire of the Lord as to the line of action that needed to be taken. By analysis, it doesn't look like the people were ready to face their enemy combatants or were they expecting such an attack. As they poured their hearts to the Lord, a prophecy came that assured them of the Lord's victory – they didn't have to fight the battle as the Lord was going to fight for them. Aside from the army being at post and combat ready, the King set up a team of Worshippers to praise and thank God. Let see the results;

> "Now when they began to sing and to praise, the Lord set ambushes against the people of Ammon, Moab, and Mount Seir, who had come against Judah; and they were defeated. For the people of Ammon and Moab stood up against the inhabitants of Mount Seir to utterly kill and destroy them. And when they had made an end of the

inhabitants of Seir, they helped to destroy one another. So when Judah came to a place overlooking the wilderness, they looked toward the multitude; and there were their dead bodies, fallen on the earth. No one had escaped. When Jehoshaphat and his people came to take away their spoil, they found among them an abundance of valuables on the dead bodies,[d]and precious jewelry, which they stripped off for themselves, more than they could carry away; and they were three days gathering the spoil because there was so much." (2 Chronicles 20:22-25)

In the end they didn't have to fight in the battle as the Lord promised. As they praised God in advance of what He had promised, He accomplished what He said He'll do. We could employ praise, thanksgiving and worship as real weapons of warfare against our spirit enemies and win because when Yahweh is attracted by our praise and inhabits it, things happen.

We have a similar story in the New Testament of Paul and Silas who had been imprisoned, because they had cast out a demon from a slave girl who had the spirit of divination and was used by her slave masters in making money telling fortunes. Whilst at the prison around midnight they started praising God and in that process, the Lord caused a shaking of the jail where they were kept, the doors opened and they walked out (Acts 16:25-34). The power of praise!

EPILOGUE

Every life ever lived has been with its fair share of adversity and even limits set on it. And your life would not be an exception. The difficulties and limits may be self-imposed due to certain mistakes and bad choices; society also imposes limitations through expectations of people or even its accepted norms of behaviour and beliefs systems, or even imposed by demon spirit entities. How you handle adversity and the resolve to pass limits on your life would determine how your life turns out. The story of the disabled beggar's encounter with the Apostles John and Peter is a typical case study with a lot to glean and to learn. We analysed the story from three different perspectives; the view to the Apostles through whom the healing came, the disabled beggar and the reader of the story. As it was, the disabled's begging for alms was only a way to manage His adversity created by the limitation of his disability, and the indication is that many of us fight so hard to get through various difficulties but ignore the underlying limitation, only to fight another day from the same fundamental source.

Through the highlights provided by the story, the whole encounter occurred because the Apostles were going up to pray in the temple. We discovered that when confronted with adversity, it becomes necessary to go up mentally, physically and spiritually. It is at that level that one can assess the difficulty and the limits in their right proportions from that high place to confront and overcome them.

The charge from the Apostles, to the disabled beggar to look at them was part of the process to bringing him the healing which was the result. They had to shift his attention from himself to themselves to mentally recondition him to see what he could be. The fact that all he sees in himself is not all that there is and could be like them in some way. We all need new mental pictures of where we want to be or what our lives could be to follow in that trajectory of imagination till we get to the destination of that realisation.

When they realised the disabled beggar had complied with their instructions, they delivered the healing to him in the name of Jesus Christ of Nazareth. When they had prayed, immediately the power of God touched the beggar and absolved the disability with all its effects. There is no name given for our comfort in our time of adversity and battling limitations other than thename of Jesus. There is so much power in the name of Jesus and even more when we have a personal relationship with Christ. God honours His son for anything His son is called upon. Jesus' name is above all else.

In the end, when the power of God had touched the beggar, he still sat until he was helped to stand by the Apostles. On so many occasions we find ourselves seated when we should be standing because we haven't got the faith to take advantage of the opportunities handed to us. It may be because sometimes we suffer adversity for so long that we are unsure of ourselves if we could stand and move forward in life. Everything set and done, the disabled runs into the temple to showcase what the Lord through the Apostles have done in his life through praise and thanksgiving.

There is no doubt that your adversity has no permanent status in your life no matter how long and arduous it has been or would be. By the power in the name of Jesus, you would come out through the breaking of the underlying limitation. It is the reason, in case you doubt if you would ever get through what you may be going through in your life, remember it did not look like there was hope for the disabled beggar who relied on people to get by in life until he met the Apostles. His life changed forever. It is up to you to make yourself available to the help of God through Jesus Christ. The practicability of fulfilling your purpose on earth, which is the measure of your success or otherwise as a human, is ultimately God's prerogative and not human projections, forecasts or soulish desires.

Remember this, that anytime you go through adversity and stand firm in the end there is not only a restoration but a double fold restitution. The Job of the scriptures went through adversity, and in the end, God gave him a double of everything he lost. Let the scripture below inspire you;

> *"You have caused men to ride over our heads;*
> *We went through fire and through water; But*
> *You brought us out to rich fulfillment."*
> *(Psalm 66:12)*

For whatever your story is, and no matter the pain you would come to a place of rich fulfilment in Christ. The place of rest from your adversity and limit in your life.